W9-BPS-366

The Iowa Caucuses
and the
Presidential Nominating Process

The Iowa Caucuses
and the
Presidential Nominating Process

EDITED BY

Peverill Squire

Westview Press
BOULDER, SAN FRANCISCO, & LONDON

Westview Special Studies in American Government and Politics

Published in 1989 in the United States of America by Westview Press, Inc., 5500 Central Avenue, Boulder, Colorado 80301, and in the United Kingdom by Westview Press, Inc., 13 Brunswick Centre, London, WC1N 1AF, England

Library of Congress Cataloging-in-Publication Data
The Iowa caucuses and the presidential nominating process/edited by
   Peverill Squire.
      p. cm. — (Westview special studies in American government
and politics)
   Includes bibliographical references.
   ISBN 0-8133-7712-9
   1. Primaries—Iowa. 2. Presidents—United States—Nomination.
I. Squire, Peverill. II. Series.
JK2075.I82I69 1989
324.5'2—dc20   89-33755
                                                                      CIP

Printed and bound in the United States of America

The paper used in this publication meets the requirements of the American National Standard for Permanence of Paper for Printed Library Materials Z39.48-1984.

10   9   8   7   6   5   4   3   2   1

For my favorite native Iowans,
L. E. Peverill and *Russell A. Squire*

Contents

Acknowledgments

The strength of any edited book lies in its contributors. The intent of this volume was to better explain the Iowa caucuses, both as a single event and as an important component in a larger system. Whatever success is achieved in meeting this goal is due to the scholars whose work appears within. The comments of Richard F. Fenno, Jr., and Marie-France Toinet helped hone the chapters. I thank Joel Barkan, who as chairman of the University of Iowa's Department of Political Science encouraged me to use money from the department's Benjamin F. Shambaugh fund for this volume, and his successor, Douglas Madsen, for help in putting it together. Karen Stewart handled the paperwork details with her usual expertise.

The first six chapters presented here are updated versions of the papers presented at a Shambaugh conference, "First in the Nation: Iowa and the Nomination Process," held at the University of Iowa, February 7–8, 1988. The last two chapters were added when their authors generously consented to extend their comments on the original papers.

On a personal note, I would like to dedicate this book to my favorite native Iowans: my grandfather, L. E. Peverill, and my son, Russell A. Squire. I hope I can give to the latter the love of politics that I gained from the former.

Peverill Squire

1

Iowa and the Nomination Process

Peverill Squire

Since Iowa's admission to the Union in 1846 the state's political parties have, with one exception, employed a caucus system to select delegates to the national convention.[1] But, what was once a contest of only marginal interest to the presidential candidates and the national media has, in recent years, become a major event in the nomination process. How has a state which in most other regards has become progressively less influential in national politics become so prominent in the single most important nationwide election?

In this chapter I examine the Iowa caucuses. First I discuss how the caucuses went from obscurity to fame, and document their importance by examining media coverage of them. The discussion then shifts to the effect the importance of the caucuses has on the behavior of candidates. The final topic addressed is the role of the caucuses in the nomination process; whether it is a function that should or should not be given to Iowa.

How Iowa Became "First in the Nation"

Iowa's "first in the nation" position did not result from skillful manipulation by its political leaders but as the unanticipated consequence of a series of unrelated decisions by the parties and the state legislature. A 1969 state law required that both parties hold their caucuses before the second Monday in May, which posed no problem because in previous years the parties had been holding them in March or April. The decision by the state Democratic party to move its 1972 caucus to late January was prompted by the early July 9 date set by the Democratic National Committee for the start of the national convention. The rules governing the Iowa Democratic party required 30 days between official party meetings—precinct caucuses, county conventions, congressional district

1

conventions, state statutory convention, state presidential convention, and the national convention—therefore January 24 was the last day the precinct caucuses could be held.[2] The 30-day rule had been adopted for practical reasons; party workers needed that time to process paper work in preparation for the next function.

The increased importance enjoyed by the Democratic caucuses which the shift to the beginning of the 1972 campaign calendar—before even the New Hampshire primary—produced came mainly from hindsight. The Democratic state party chairman at the time, Clif Larson, recalls (Lehr, 1988, p. 12), "We didn't realize it at first, but we figured it out . . . But even then we didn't anticipate the attention we got." The caucuses that year did receive some national media coverage and visits from the candidates which they had not gotten before. But the actual amount of attention was slight; McGovern, for example, was in the state only a day and a half (Cook, 1987, p. 8) before his "surprise" showing in the caucuses.[3] The network evening news shows had some coverage of the caucuses the day after they were held, but none leading up to them.[4]

The caucus results seem to have become important only in retrospect, when it became necessary to pinpoint the beginning of the McGovern surge.[5] But their contribution to his victory can be exaggerated. Books written following the 1972 campaign (e.g. White, 1973; Crouse, 1973) make no mention of the Iowa caucuses. They were the first event of the election year, and therefore worthy of some attention, but they were not deemed important at the time by most observers.

The small amount of national attention that the caucuses had received was, however, noted by the leadership of the state's parties. The Republicans had not benefited because they had held their caucuses in April. The two parties saw cooperation to be in their best interests and they reached an agreement to hold their 1976 caucuses on the same date—January 19. The goal was, of course, to keep the caucuses first on the campaign calendar and receive the substantial amount of attention from the media and candidates warranted by that position. The GOP even changed their procedures, instituting a poll of caucus participants, so that they would have "results" to give the media.[6] The Democratic state party chairman at the time, Tom Whitney, claims that his party actively courted attention (Lehr, 1988, p. 13):

> We convinced the candidates that the most important place to be was in Iowa because that's where the media was going to be. We convinced the media that if you were going to report the story you had to be here because the candidates were.

But, while the state parties positioned the caucuses to be more consequential in the nomination process, it was Jimmy Carter's successful drive to the 1976 Democratic nomination that made them important. The astute plan developed by Hamilton Jordan to exploit the changed rules under which the Democratic nomination was contested gave great weight to the results in Iowa. The Carter campaign was banking on extensive national media coverage, therefore they concentrated many of their limited resources in Iowa. When the results of straw polls in Iowa during the fall were given coverage in the *New York Times* and other national media the Carter strategy was validated (Witcover, 1977, pp. 214–215).

Several other candidates, however, did not anticipate the increased importance of Iowa. Morris Udall, in particular, had to readjust his tactics to give more attention to the caucuses (Arterton, 1978a, pp. 15–17). He had initially intended to downplay them in favor of the New Hampshire primary, but by the late fall of 1975 he and his advisors realized the necessity of making an effort to do well in Iowa. His belated attempt fell short, a failure many suggest did great damage to his chances for the nomination.

Thus it is in 1976 that the Iowa caucuses really achieved national stature in that they were acknowledged by many participants and elite observers as being important *before they occurred*. The fact that Carter used the caucuses as a springboard to the nomination ensured that candidates in succeeding elections would make great efforts to perform well in them.

The Importance of the Iowa Caucuses: 1976–1988

The Iowa caucuses became significant in 1976, and their importance has continued to increase. Accounts of more recent nomination campaigns give great weight to the role of the caucuses (e.g. Witcover, 1977; Germond and Witcover, 1981; Harwood, 1980; Polsby, 1985). Further evidence supporting this contention is given in Table 1.1, which compares the amount of coverage given to the caucuses by the *New York Times* and the television network evening news programs. The *Times* did not carry a single story on the caucuses in 1975 and it printed only 7 in 1976—a year where both parties had nomination races. The *Times* published 16 articles on the caucuses in 1983 and 42 in 1984, despite the fact only the Democratic nomination was contested. The trend toward increased coverage has continued. In *1987* the *Times* had 69 caucus stories, with another 36 appearing in 1988.

The figures for coverage on the network evening news programs are just as striking. No stories were broadcast in 1975 and just 15 were shown in 1976. The day after the 1976 caucuses the networks spent from 3 minutes (ABC) to 6 minutes (NBC) reporting the results. The 1984 contest received far more attention. Only 1 caucus story was shown in 1983, but 46 were aired in 1984. All three network news programs made Iowa their lead story both the day of the caucuses and the day after them, averaging 10 minutes on the caucuses the first night and 7 minutes the next evening. The simple conclusion to draw from Table 1.1 is that the caucuses receive extensive attention from the national media, and that the reporting of events in Iowa has increased over time. Moreover, as several studies (e.g. Robinson and Sheehan, 1983; Adams, 1984, 1987; Buell, 1987a) have documented, the Iowa caucuses get as much attention as the New Hampshire primary and far more coverage than delegate selection contests in most other states.

The result of this intensive coverage is not to make Iowa a "king maker" but rather a "peasant maker." Candidates who finish first are not guaranteed the nomination, as evidenced by George Bush in 1980, or Robert Dole and Richard Gephardt in 1988. But, candidates who do not do well by finishing among the leaders are doomed. Before 1988, no one who had finished below second place in Iowa since 1972 had gotten his party's nomination.[7] In the most recent contest, Dukakis and Bush were able to survive their third place showings for a couple of reasons. First, although two other candidates gained more votes, both Dukakis and Bush received a respectable level of support—each got a higher percentage of the vote than did Gary Hart in his 1984 second place showing. Second, both Bush and Dukakis were well-known, well-organized, and well-funded in New Hampshire, where overwhelming victories eight days after Iowa allowed them to project the image of a winner.

Even in 1988, however, the Iowa caucus results culled the field in each party. Several candidates—Babbitt, Hart, du Pont and Kemp—never recovered from their poor performances in Iowa. The dynamics behind this reduction in the number of viable candidate are well established (e.g. Polsby, 1983; Bartels, 1985; Matthews, 1978; Arterton, 1978b). Because of the extensive media coverage and the subsequent "winnowing" of the field those seeking their party's nomination must do well in Iowa.[8]

Given the importance attached to the caucus results by the media it is not surprising to find that the behavior of candidates has been influenced. As the media gives more attention and meaning to the results in Iowa candidates have found it necessary to spend more time and money campaigning in the state. Table 1.2 presents figures on the number of visits to Iowa made by candidates and the amount of money spent

TABLE 1.1   Number of Stories on the 1976, 1984 and 1988 Iowa Caucuses in the *New York Times* and on the Network News

Year	New York Times	Network News
1975	0	0
1976	7	15
1983	16	1
1984	42	46
1987	69	
1988	49	

Source: *New York Times Index* and *Television News Index* for given years.

TABLE 1.2   Number of Days and Amount of Money Spent by Candidates in Iowa: 1976 and 1987-88

Candidate		Days	Money
1976	Republicans		
	Ford	0	
	Reagan	2	
	Mean	1	66,047
	Democrats		
	Brown	0	
	Carter	7	
	Church	0	
	Jackson	3	
	Udall	10	
	Wallace	0	
	Mean	3	49,021
1987-88	Republicans		
	Bush	16	234,000[a]
	Dole	31	229,000
	Du Pont	62	97,000
	Haig	21	18,000
	Kemp	49	149,000
	Robertson	22	201,000
	Mean	50	155,000
	Democrats		
	Babbitt	80	296,000
	Dukakis	46	214,000
	Gephardt	87	249,000
	Gore	26	114,000
	Jackson	30	47,000
	Simon	53	134,000
	Mean	78	176,000

[a]Information collected prior to October, 1987.

Source: 1976 data from Aldrich (1980, pp. 226, 228, 232, 233); 1987-88 data from *Campaign Scorecard* (1987) and *Campaign Scorecard* (1988).

in the state by them in 1976 and in 1988. The 1976 numbers, compiled by Aldrich (1980, pp. 226–233), show that Udall spent 10 days in Iowa, Carter 7 days, and Henry Jackson just 3 days. On the Republican side Ronald Reagan was in Iowa 2 days and President Gerald Ford did not visit the state as a candidate. While these numbers may not include a number of trips made to Iowa by the candidates well before the caucuses— particularly for Carter—they do give a strong impression of how important the state was thought to be at the time.

These figures contrast sharply with those compiled by the *Des Moines Register* for the 1988 campaign ("Campaign Scorecard," 1988). By the day of the caucuses Democratic candidates had spent a mean of 78 days in the state; their Republican counterparts had averaged 50 days. Both Richard Gephardt and Bruce Babbitt spent over 100 days campaigning in Iowa and several other candidates came close to that number.

Campaign spending figures demonstrate the same increase in importance attached to Iowa by those contesting the nominations. Aldrich's 1976 data show that declared Democratic candidates spent an average of just over $49,000 in the state, while Ford and Reagan spent around $66,000 each to contest the caucuses. In 1987, *with over three months still to go* ("Campaign Scorecard," 1987), Democrats had spent an average of $176,000 and Republicans, $155,000.

Contestants for each party's nomination have also taken to trying to win support by directing contributions from their political action committees to campaigns of state politicians. The sums given in 1986 were not trivial. As shown in Table 1.3, nearly $150,000 was contributed by presidential candidates to those seeking the governorship, statewide offices and state legislative seats in that election. One candidate, Bruce Babbitt, even loaned staff members to a few Democratic campaigns. The idea behind this munificence is, of course, to gain support from state politicians and to use their backing to develop a strong organization.

Thus there is little question about the importance of the Iowa caucuses in the nominations process. National media give the caucuses an enormous amount of coverage, and the candidates lavish the state with attention. The remaining question is whether Iowa, or any state, deserves this role.

The Iowa Caucuses and the Nomination Process

The prominence of the Iowa caucuses has led a number of political observers and a few candidates to suggest that something is wrong with the nomination system—an act referred to in the state as "Iowa bashing" (e.g. Hyde, 1987). These detractors support their claims in a number of ways. First, they note that the state is unrepresentative demographically. As can be seen in Table 1.4, there is evidence to support this position.

TABLE 1.3   Campaign Contributions from Presidential Candidates to Candidates in Iowa
State Elections in 1986

Candidate	Governor	Statewide Office	Legislature
Republicans			
Bush	10,000	7,720	24,450
Dole	5,000	5,000	4,090
Kemp	5,000	4,000	6,800
Rumsfeld	0	500	1,250
Democrats			
Babbitt	10,000	0	15,100
Biden	30,807	3,303	5,600
Gephardt	9,000	0	0

Source: Norman (1986).

TABLE 1.4   Comparisons between Iowa and the Nation

Candidate	Iowa	United States
Population	2,884,000	238,740,000
Population Density	52	67
Percent Black	1.4	11.7
Over 65 Years	14.1	11.9
Crime Rate (per 100,000)	3,800	5,031
Unemployment Rate (1984)	7.0	7.5
Divorce Rate	3.7	5.0
Abortion Rate (per 1000)	12.6	28.8
Social Security Rate (per 1000) (1983)	172.5	150.5
Public Assistance (% of population)	4.8	6.2
AFDC (% children under 18)	8.7	11.2
% Completing High School	71.5	66.5
Newspaper Circulation (per capita)	.278	.268

Source: State and Metropolitan Area Data Book (1986).

The state has a higher percentage of older citizens, and fewer minorities and metropolitan area residents than the national average. It also has lower rates of unemployment, crime, divorce and abortion. A lower percentage of the population is on Public Assistance or AFDC, a higher percentage draw social security. The state exceeds the national mean in the percentage of the population that has graduated from high school and in per capita newspaper circulation.

The rebuttal to this general line of argument is that every state deviates from the national mean on some number of important characteristics. That Iowa does as well is only important if it can be demonstrated that these differences have political consequences. That is, are the candidates chosen by Iowans attending the caucuses different from those who would be chosen by other means?

One way to address this question is to see whether the choices Iowans make on caucus night differ from those held by the nation at that time. Table 1.5 gives the last national Gallup Poll data prior to the caucuses, and the results of the caucuses. In the seven contested races from 1976 to 1988 there are several instances where Iowans deviated significantly— Carter in 1976 and Gephardt in 1988 in Democratic contests and Bush in the 1980 and Dole in 1988 Republican races. The other three times— Ford in 1976, Carter in 1980 and Mondale in 1984—the votes of Iowans closely reflected national preferences.

Closer examination of Table 1.5 reveals the deviations are not as striking as they might seem. Carter, for instance, had little support nationally before the caucuses, but the first three choices of the Gallup respondents were not active candidates. Thus Carter jumped out of a pack that was, with the exception of Henry Jackson, not nationally known. If it had not been Carter, it might just as well have been another unknown candidate. Moreover, Carter finished behind "uncommitted" suggesting Iowa Democrats, like their national peers, preferred Humphrey, Wallace, McGovern or some other person not in the race. The situation in 1988 was similarly unsettled, with no dominant nationally known contestant in the race, and the added complications of the Jackson and resurrected Hart candidacies. Given the situation the results of that election are not strikingly out of line with national sentiments.

On the Republican side Bush surprised observers with his showing in 1980, but national favorite Reagan finished a very close second and the other Republicans received support roughly equivalent to their Gallup figures. Similarly, in 1988 Bush was shocked by Dole, but the Senator from Kansas received support comparable to national figures.

Another complaint, one registered by Democrats, is that a state which has voted for their party's candidate only twice in the last ten elections— Johnson in 1964 and Dukakis in 1988—should not be given so much

TABLE 1.5   National Preferences and Iowa Caucus Results (in percent)

Candidate	Pre-Caucus Gallup Poll	Iowa Caucus
1976 Democrats		
Humphrey	29[a]	–[b]
Wallace	20	–
McGovern	10	–
Jackson	9	1
Muskie	6	–
Bayh	5	13
Shriver	5	3
Other, DK	16	
Carter		28
Harris		10
Udall		6
Uncommitted		37
Republicans		
Ford	53	45
Reagan	42	43
Undecided	5	11
1980 Democrats		
Carter	51[c]	59[d]
Kennedy	37	31
Undecided	12	10
Republicans		
Reagan	40	29
Ford	18	–
Connally	9	9
Baker	9	16
Bush	7	32
Dole	4	2
Other, DK		
Crane		7
Anderson		4
Undecided		2

Continued

TABLE 1.5 Continued

Candidate		Pre-Caucus Gallup Poll		Iowa Caucus
1984	Democrats			
	Mondale	49[e]		49[f]
	Glenn	13		4
	Jackson	13		2
	McGovern	5		10
	Askew	3		3
	Cranston	3		10
	Hart	3		17
	Hollings	1		0
	None, DK	11		
	Uncommitted			10
1988	Democrats			
	Hart	—[g]	(30)[h]	0[j]
	Jackson	22	(20)	9
	Dukakis	14	(15)	22
	Simon	8	(8)	27
	Gore	7	(5)	0
	Gephardt	5	(2)	31
	Babbitt	1	(2)	6
	Uncommitted			5
	Republicans			
	Bush	47	(44)	19
	Dole	22	(35)	37
	Robertson	7		25
	Kemp	4		11
	Haig	4		0
	Du Pont	1		7

[a]January 2-5, 1976.
[b]January 19, 1976.
[c]January 4-6, 1980.
[d]January 21, 1980.
[e]February 10-13, 1984.
[f]February 20, 1984.
[g]October 23-26, 1987.
[h]ABC/Washington Post Poll, December 15-18, 1987.
[j]February 8, 1988.

Sources: *The Gallup Poll, Public Opinion 1984*; *Public Opinion* (1988).

influence over who becomes their standard-bearer. There are a number of weaknesses in this argument. First, since 1972, when the nomination rules changes went into effect, only the District of Columbia has voted for the Democratic candidate in all five elections, and only Minnesota—Iowa's northern neighbor—has backed the party's ticket in four elections![9] Iowa has, in fact, been among the states most supportive of Democratic presidential candidates. As Table 1.6 shows, Iowans have either reflected the national vote, or been more in favor of the Democrat than the national mean. Second, while during this time period the Republicans have controlled the state's governorship, Democrats have held Senate and House seats and, much of the time, have been in the majority in both houses of the state legislature. More Iowans are registered as Democrats than as Republicans (Cook, 1987, p. 120).[10] The state is now competitive between the two parties with the Democrats holding the edge (Squire, forthcoming). Finally, in 1976, when Iowans did deviate from national preferences in the Democratic candidate they supported, they started Jimmy Carter on his way to the White House—the only Democrat to win that office since 1964! Evidence does not seem to support the notion that Iowa is too Republican to play a prominent role in Democratic affairs.

Some Democrats also criticize Iowa on the grounds that those who participate in the party's caucuses are too liberal, giving support to candidates who are too far to the left to be successful in the general election. The results of past caucuses belie this notion. Iowa Democrats preferred Muskie to McGovern, Carter to a number of liberals, Carter to Kennedy, and Gephardt to Simon. Only in 1984 did they support a liberal, Walter Mondale, who was also the overwhelming choice of Democrats nationally. If there is a valid complaint that the caucuses back liberal candidates it is in the *Republican* party, where Reagan lost close races to Ford in 1976 and Bush in 1980.

Finally, the caucuses are assailed on the more general grounds that too few people participate in them to be representative. As can be seen in Table 1.7, no certain turnout figures exist. Rough calculations of participation rates in the 1976, 1980 and 1984 caucuses by registered Democrats and Republicans puts the figures between 14 and 20 percent.[11] These numbers are impressive for caucuses (cf. Ranney, 1977, p. 16) and approach turnout levels in some primaries (cf. Ranney, 1972, p. 24; Ranney, 1977, p. 20). As a device for allowing mass participation in the democratic process the Iowa caucuses seem to fare as well as the less time consuming and less demanding primaries.

Thus many of the charges leveled at the caucuses do not seem well founded. The choices made by Iowans who attend the caucuses are not particularly different from the preferences of their party identifiers

12

TABLE 1.6   General Election Results: Iowa and the Nation (in percent)

Year	Iowa	Nation
1972		
Nixon (R)	59	61
McGovern (D)	41	38
1976		
Ford (R)	51	48
Carter (D)	49	50
1980		
Reagan (R)	52	51
Carter (D)	39	41
Anderson	9	7
1984		
Reagan (R)	54	59
Mondale (D)	46	41
1988		
Bush (R)	45	54
Dukakis (D)	55	46

TABLE 1.7   Participation in the Iowa Caucuses, 1972 to 1988

Year	Democrats (Estimated)	Republicans (Estimated)
1972	20,000[a] 60,000[b]	
1976	38,500[abc]	20,000[a]
1980	100,000[acd]	106,051[ac] 115,000[d]
1984	75,000[ac] 85,000[d]	
1988	120,000[e]	110,000[e]

[a]figures reported in Cook (1987, p. 11).
[b]figures reported in Maisel (1987, p. 66).
[c]figures reported in Winebrenner (1985).
[d]figures reported in *Iowa Official Register, 1985-86.*
[e]figures reported in "Iowa's Star's Take a Back Seat in New Hampshire" (1988).

nationally. Participation levels are not notably different. If any state is to be given sole possession of the first spot on the election calendar Iowa is as good a choice as any.[12]

The question then becomes not whether Iowa should be first but whether having any single state first is good for the political process. On the one hand, a nomination system where candidates make multiple trips to a particular state far in advance of the election, as happened in Iowa during the most recent campaign (e.g. Yepsen, 1985a, b, c, d), may discourage many attractive candidates from entering the race. Putting presidential hopefuls in the position of spending their "vacations" bicycling across the state (Yepsen, 1986), or visiting all 99 of the state's counties may not provide voters much insight into the kind of chief executive particular candidates might make.[13] On the other hand, in a "mixed system" of the sort advocated by Polsby (1983) the caucuses provide information about the appeal of candidates when voters can give them close scrutiny which is unlikely to be produced by other delegate selection procedures.

If we accept the proposition that the current system is flawed, what are the alternatives to it? As I have argued, Iowa is as good a choice as any state to start the process, so substituting another state does not seem to be a satisfying answer. Other proposals suggest a series of regional primaries, or a single national primary, ideas which also have flaws (e.g. Ranney, 1978; Polsby and Wildavsky, 1984, pp. 223–241) because, among other problems, they are biased in favor of well-known and well-financed candidates.

The main point to keep in mind is that there is no perfect system which is guaranteed to produce ideal candidates. The current system has problems—too much power is given to Iowa and New Hampshire to narrow the field of candidates. Chances are, however, that little will be done to change the current rules under which both parties contest their nominations. The battles which were fought over which state would come first in 1988 (Buell, 1987b) have probably settled the issue for sometime to come. Even before the 1988 caucuses the respected Democratic party insider Robert Strauss—an Iowa critic—commented, ". . . if we have another reform commission I might take the gas pipe."[14] A pre-convention suggestion by Jesse Jackson to diminish the importance of the caucuses was dropped as part of an agreement with Dukakis regarding the rules governing the 1992 campaign (Hyde, 1988). Given the strong possibility that Iowa will remain "first in the nation" for the foreseeable future it is important that we better understand the system as it exists, a task undertaken in the following chapters.

Notes

1. The exception was 1916 when a primary was used. The following discussion of the evolution of the Iowa caucuses to 1972 relies on Winebrenner (1983, 1985). See also Schier (1980) and Mayer (1987, pp. 20–21).

2. The Iowa caucuses are a four-tiered process. The initial event is the precinct caucuses which are widely covered by the media. The precinct caucuses elect delegates to the 99 county conventions, which then select delegates to the six congressional district conventions, which in turn elect representatives to the state convention. A somewhat different version of the events leading to the movement of the Democratic caucuses to the begining of the election calendar is given in Lehr (1988).

3. Winebrenner (1985, p. 107) reports McGovern was in the state for three days. McGovern's surprise finish was behind Muskie and uncommitted. See Table 1.5 for the actual results.

4. On January 25, 1972, CBS and NBC spent 4 minutes and ABC 2 minutes discussing the results and the delays in obtaining them, and on the reforms in the Democratic party. The next day CBS gave 30 seconds to reviewing the results, the other networks made no mention of them.

5. Witcover (1977, p. 213) observes, "In 1972 the rise of George McGovern's barely detected grass-roots efforts at the precinct level had been overlooked for a considerable time by the major newspapers and the television networks; their focus was squarely on Muskie. . . . Not even McGovern's show of strength in Iowa shook that perception, and only in retrospect was it realized that something significant had been building for McGovern out in the country." The same basic point is made by Mayer (1987, pp. 20–21), who notes that politicians in New Hampshire were unaware that Iowa had supplanted their first in the nation status.

6. The Republicans employ a voting procedure at the precinct level which does not translate well into either overall voter preferences or candidate delegate totals. Using a preference poll provides the party information of interest to the media. In 1976 these data were generated by a survey of 62 precincts. In 1980 all precincts were polled.

7. The examples are numerous. Among them are Udall and Henry Jackson in 1976, John Connally and Robert Dole in 1980, and John Glenn in 1984. Note, however, what is being discussed is rank order among the candidates—in 1976, for example, uncommitted votes outnumbered those for Carter, but little attention was given to that result.

8. In his discussion of the New Hampshire primary, Mayer (1987, p. 23) observers, "The 'winnowing' function . . . is now performed almost entirely by the Iowa caucuses."

9. The Republicans have won at least the last five presidential contests in a number of states, including New Hampshire, Connecticut, New Jersey, Michigan, Illinois, Colorado, and California. Also, it must be noted that Mondale was on the ballot three times his native Minnesota voted for the Democratic ticket.

10. The specific figures are 35 percent Democrats, 31 percent Republicans and 33 other (primarily independents). See also Squire (forthcoming).

11. These calculations were made using the voter registration figures for 1987 given in Cook (1980, p. 120). Given the state's slightly declining population during the last decade using these figures for previous years is reasonable.

12. This can be argued without any reference to less empirical and more metaphysical qualities, like civility, goodness and honesty, that Iowans are purported to possess.

13. Candidates do visit almost every city of any size in the state with one exception: West Branch. The site of Herbert Hoover's birthplace and presidential library is bypassed by Republicans and Democrats alike (Carlson, 1987).

14. Others are resigned to Iowa's leadership role. For example, Don Fowler, who headed the last Democratic reform commission, has commented (Hyde, 1987), "The truth is we've tried to soften the impact of Iowa and New Hampshire and it's never worked. Let me put it this way: As long as Iowa and New Hampshire insist on having their events early, and as long as the candidates continue to go there, there's not much the Democratic Party can do about it."

References

Adams, William C. 1984. Media Coverage of Campaign '84. *Public Opinion*, 7: 9–13.

_____. 1987. As New Hampshire Goes . . . In Gary R. Orren and Nelson W. Polsby, eds., *Media and Momentum*. Chatham, NJ: Chatham House Publishers, Inc.

Aldrich, John H. 1980. *Before the Convention*. Chicago: University of Chicago Press.

Arterton, F. Christopher. 1978a. Campaign Organizations Confront the Media-Political Environment. In James David Barber, ed., *Race for the Presidency*. Englewood Cliffs, NJ: Prentice-Hall, Inc.

_____. 1978b. The Media Politics of Presidential Campaigns: A Study of the Carter Nomination Drive. In James David Barber, ed., *Race for the Presidency*. Englewood Cliffs, N.J.: Prentice–Hall, Inc.

Bartels, Larry M. 1985. Expectations and Preferences in Presidential Nominating Campaigns. *American Political Science Review*, 79: 804–815.

Buell, Emmett H. 1987a. Locals and Cosmopolitans: National, Regional and State Newspaper Coverage of the New Hampshire Primary. In Gary R. Orren and Nelson W. Polsby, eds., *Media and Momentum*. Chatham, N.J.: Chatham House Publishers, Inc.

_____. 1987b. First-in-the-Nation: Disputes Over the Timing of Early Democratic Presidential Primaries and Caucuses in 1984 and 1988. *The Journal of Law & Politics*, 4: 311–342.

Campaign Scorecard. November 1, 1987. *Des Moines Register*.

_____. February 7, 1988. *Des Moines Register*.

Carlson, John. December 20, 1987. Ghost of the Depression Spooks Candidates. *Des Moines Register*.

Cook, Rhodes. 1987. *Race for the Presidency*. Washington D.C.: Congressional Quarterly, Inc.

Crouse, Timothy. 1973. *The Boys on the Bus.* New York: Random House.

Germond, Jack W., and Jules Witcover. 1981. *Blue Smoke and Mirrors.* New York: Viking Press.

Harwood, Richard, ed., 1980. *The Pursuit of the Presidency 1980.* New York: Berkley Publishing Co.

Hyde, John. December 6, 1987. Rising Chorus of Complaint on Caucuses. *Des Moines Register.*

————. June 26, 1988. Jackson Drops Call to Change Iowa Caucuses. *Des Moines Register.*

Iowa's Stars Take a Back Seat in New Hampshire. 1988. *Congressional Quarterly Weekly Report,* 46:287–290.

Lehr, Jeff. 1988. Iowa's Primary Caucus. *The Iowa Alumni Review,* 41: 12-13.

Maisel, L. Sandy. 1987. *Parties and Elections in America.* New York: Random House.

Matthews, Donald R. 1978. Winnowing: The News Media and the 1976 Presidential Nominations. In James David Barber. ed., *Race for the Presidency.* Englewood Cliffs, N.J.: Prentice-Hall, Inc.

Mayer, William G. 1987. The New Hampshire Primary: A Historical Overview. In Gary R. Orren and Nelson W. Polsby, eds., *Media and Momentum.* Chatham, NJ: Chatham House Publishers, Inc.

Norman, Jane. November 23, 1986. Caucuses a Windfall for State Politicians. *Des Moines Register.*

Polsby, Nelson W. 1983. *Consequences of Party Reform.* New York: Oxford University Press.

————. 1985. The Democratic Nomination and the Evolution of the Party System. In Austin Ranney, ed., *The American Elections of 1984.* Durham, N.C.: Duke University Press.

————, and Aaron Wildavsky. 1984. *Presidential Elections,* 6th ed. New York: Charles Scribner's Sons.

Ranney, Austin. 1972. Turnout and Representation in Presidential Primary Elections. *American Political Science Review,* 66: 21–37.

————. 1977. *Participation in American Presidential Nominations 1976.* Washington, D.C.: AEI.

————. 1978. *The Federalization of Presidential Primaries.* Washington, D.C.: AEI.

Robinson, Michael J., and Margaret Sheehan. 1983. *Over the Wire and on TV.* New York: Russell Sage Foundation.

Schier, Steven E. 1980. *The Rules of the Game: Democratic National Convention Delegate Selection in Iowa and Wisconsin.* Washington D.C.: University Press of America.

Squire, Peverill. Forthcoming. Iowa and the Drift to the Democrats. In Maureen Moakley, ed., *Party Realignment in the American States.* Columbus, OH: Ohio State University Press.

White, Theodore H. 1973. *The Making of the President 1972.* New York: Atheneum.

Winebrenner, Hugh. 1983. The Evolution of the Iowa Precinct Caucuses. *The Annals of Iowa,* 46: 618–35.

————. 1985. The Iowa Precinct Caucuses: The Making of a Media Event. *Southeastern Political Review,* 13:99–132.

Witcover, Jules. 1977. *Marathon.* New York: Signet.

Yepsen, David. 1985a. Trade Barriers No Solution, GOP Hopeful Kemp Says. *Des Moines Register,* September 14.

_____. 1985b. Deficit Attacked by Democratic Hopeful in D.M. *Des Moines Register,* September 30.

_____. 1985c. Kemp Cites Need for Judges Against Abortion. *Des Moines Register,* October 6.

_____. 1985d. Delaware Senator Opens Fire on Presidential Race. *Des Moines Register,* November 3.

_____. July 20, 1986. Babbitt Hopes Bike Ride Gets His Campaign in Gear. *Des Moines Register.*

2

How Representative Are the Iowa Caucuses?

Walter J. Stone, Alan I. Abramowitz, and Ronald B. Rapoport

The importance of representation in the contemporary presidential selection process seems almost self-evident. Groups of decision-makers "act for" or "stand for" others in selecting a presidential nominee (Pitkin, 1967). Certainly the national party conventions in some sense represent their national parties by formally selecting the nominee. Thus, a concern of scholars and party reformers alike has been with the descriptive match between convention delegates and the party's popular base. A number of studies have applied concepts related to representation to the study of national convention delegates (Kirkpatrick, 1975, 1976; McClosky, et al., 1960; Miller and Jennings, 1986, are prominent examples). In addition to considering the national nominating conventions as representing the popular bases of their parties, one can think of various steps in the process as similarly aggregating interests. The question can then be posed whether primary voters represent the citizenry or partisans either in their state or nationally (e.g., Keeter and Zukin, 1983; Lengle, 1981; Ranney, 1972) or whether state convention delegates represent those who have participated at lower levels within the state (Hutter and Schier, 1984). Reformers and critics often suggest the current process is "unrepresentative" since it gives disproportionate influence over the outcome to atypical interests in such out of the way places as New Hampshire and Iowa. As a result, Iowa and New Hampshire attract considerable attention not only from the popular media, but also from scholars (Winebrenner, 1987; Orren and Polsby, 1987).

If the question of representation in the process is central, it also raises a number of issues which are probably impossible to address adequately. While the case can be made that primary voters, convention delegates, and caucus-goers act for others, they often do so not in the manner of a legislator who is institutionally connected to his constituents. Nonetheless, choices made by a relatively small number of nomination activists affect the interests of all citizens. Perhaps what is troubling about the process (and probably unresolvable) is that it lacks the formal, institutionalized connections of electoral accountability which structure legislative representation.

This lack of formal accountability is nowhere more apparent than when citizens in an early contest like Iowa "act for" the nation by starting the presidential sweepstakes. Iowans winnow the field. They endow credibility upon a "frontrunner" or "challenger." They have the potential to launch or retard a campaign's momentum. They dictate the ability of a campaign to command attention in the press with the resulting credibility and ability to attract resources to continue their campaign (Joslyn, 1984; Orren and Polsby, 1987).

Iowa is important in presidential politics. Jimmy Carter and Gary Hart are certainly recent examples of how "success" in the Iowa caucuses can propel a little known candidate to national prominence. Hence the question, "How representative are the Iowa caucuses?" We begin by suggesting some conceptual problems which make the question difficult to answer. In some respects these difficulties amount to alternative ways of posing the question. The second part of the paper, then, offers a data-intensive set of comparisons which speak to some of the ways the question can be posed. The third and final section of the paper addresses the question of how participants decide whom to support for their party's nomination. This analysis permits some speculation on the consequences of the comparisons undertaken.

Conceptual Difficulties

Some Sources of Distortion in the Process

It is relatively easy to list some potential sources of distortion in the nomination process. Some of these apply to almost any method of selecting a nominee while others apply with special force to analysis of the Iowa caucuses. But any analysis of representation implicitly or explicitly must confront distorting effects such as the following:

Participation Thresholds. Political participation of any sort tends to be costly in personal resources and to require predisposing attitudes (Verba and Nie, 1972). This means that participants are systematically different from nonparticipants. Primary voters are not typical of the larger pool of eligible voters. They are likely to be of a higher social status, to be more strongly committed to their party, and to be more firmly convinced of their issue positions than nonparticipants (Ranney, 1972; Keeter and

Zukin, 1983; Lengle, 1981). These findings make sense since voting in a primary election requires some effort and commitment from the individual. We could suppose that the greater the effort and commitment required—the higher the participation threshold, in other words—the greater this kind of distortion. Thus, caucus-attenders might differ from the eligible pool more than primary voters, and convention delegates might differ still more than caucus-attenders.

Campaign Effects. The campaign in Iowa is more intense than the campaigns in states like Washington, Maine or Michigan. Mostly, this is due to the agenda setting function of the Iowa contest. Campaign effects might lower the participation threshold by stimulating interest among otherwise less attentive citizens. But they may create other kinds of distortion since an Iowa campaign is more personal and more prolonged than the ordinary state campaign. The caucus-attender in Iowa who has endured a relatively prolonged and intense campaign is likely to differ in significant ways from the citizen in another state who experiences the campaign in a much more remote way.

Candidates. The candidates competing in a state can have obvious distorting effects. What choice is offered to participants? In a Democratic contest, if two liberal candidates are fighting over the same faction in the party while a third moderate or conservative candidate has no competition for that wing of the party, the results may be quite different than if the campaign involves two moderate to conservative candidates and only one liberal. Polsby (1983) discusses some of the distortion that can result from multi-candidate races competing for support among atypical participants.

Time. The attention lavished on Iowa is almost wholly because it is first. Several of the sources of distortion such as campaign effects and the menu of candidate choice offered are intimately connected to the fact Iowa is first. But presumably there is also learning that takes place through the campaign season (Markus, 1982; Bartels, 1987; Brady and Johnston, 1987). Citizens in New York or California have had longer to watch the campaign, the candidates have had more time to distinguish themselves for good or ill. These and related effects are unavoidable in a sequential process. By "acting for" New York and California primary voters, Iowa caucus-attenders inevitably affect the choices and perceptions of citizens later in the process.

The Unique Character of Iowa. Iowa is not typical of the nation. It does not have large urban centers, it has a small minority population, its culture and economy are more heavily dependent on agriculture than many states, it has a lower than average crime rate, a higher than average literacy rate, etc. Of course, any state is unique, but many critics suggest that Iowa is more atypical than most.

Perceptual Bias. The threshold effects discussed above are interesting in part because they skew the participant pool with respect to demographics, issue preferences, and other attitudes. These effects are most troubling if participants support candidates on the basis of those characteristics which differentiate them from nonparticipants. If, for example, participants choose candidates on the basis of their own ideological and issue preferences, and if those preferences do not reflect the preferences of nonparticipants, a significant bias may be introduced. Much of the early literature on convention delegates emphasized this problem because of the unrepresentative character of such activists, and because substantial proportions of convention delegates appeared to subscribe to "amateur" or "purist" norms (Wildavsky, 1965; Roback, 1975; Soule and Clarke, 1970).

Yet there is good reason to suppose participants think ahead to the general election stage of the process and base their nomination choices in part on what the general electorate is likely to want (Coleman, 1972; Aldrich, 1980). To some degree, each participant's interest in nominating a candidate likely to win in the fall election may supplant the absence of formal accountability mechanisms. But even if such considerations totally dominate candidate support calculations, there are still significant perceptual biases that can distort activists' perceptions of the general electorate's preferences. Thus, participants might easily come to believe that the most electable candidate is also the candidate whom they prefer on other grounds. Or, judgments about the general electorate's ideological preferences could result from rationalizations of the participants' own preferences.

These sources of distortion in the nomination process, taken as a whole, often are employed as the basis for supporting arguments for change and reform. Some, such as those linked to the dynamic nature of the process, would be altered dramatically by such reforms as a national primary. Others, such as the effects of participation thresholds, are probably built in to almost any conceivable process that does not include formal accountability to a broader constituency. Alternatives to the contemporary process might remedy some biases, but they would surely introduce or exacerbate others. On the supposition that any criticism of the current process should be informed about the kinds of distortion which emerge, we can proceed. However, the purpose of the analysis which follows is not to support any particular critique or alternative, nor is it designed to defend any specific aspect of the current process.

Representative of Whom?

Concepts of representation, whether they focus on compositional variables such as demographics and issue preferences, or upon the actions of representatives such as the selection of a nominee or the making of law, always imply a constituency. Who is the constituency of nomination participants? In the case of Iowa caucus attenders, what is the relevant comparison group?

One possible answer is there is no relevant comparison group because Iowa caucus-goers stand and act for no one but themselves. They are not formally accountable to anyone, nor do they pretend to represent anyone else's interests. The concern with representation springs from the fact that Iowans are first in the nomination process which means what they do affects the interests of the rest of the nation. But if they benefit in some ways from being first, there are also disadvantages which should be recognized before arguing they necessarily play a special role representing those who come after. Many Iowans make choices which ultimately are irrelevant because of what happens later in the process. Those who support their first-choice candidate only to see him or her drop out later are denied the chance of backing a more realistic alternative. Moreover, they lack the information which uniquely results from a prolonged campaign and which is therefore available to later participants. To those who suggest they have disproportionate influence over who the next president will be, Iowans may respond that the power of Californians in determining the Democratic nominee in 1972 is at least as impressive. Focusing on Iowa's influence might overemphasize the lessons of recent campaigns in which a frontrunner benefitted from momentum and locked up the nomination relatively early. In 1988, the Iowa victories of Richard Gephardt and Robert Dole appear to support a more modest view of the Hawkeye state's influence.

Despite these objections, Iowa's status means that it retains the potential to define the alternatives presented to primary voters and caucus-participants later in the process, and renders representation a question of enduring interest. What comparisons are implied by a focus on representation in this case? Certainly the comparison of caucus-attenders with the Iowa electorate is an obvious one. This will allow us to assess the degree of bias linked to caucus participation. A second comparison group is the national electorate. This comparison is relevant to the degree one thinks of participants in Iowa (or in any state) as standing for or acting instead of the national population. The bias assessed in this manner is particularly relevant to those who emphasize the atypical character of Iowa and who argue for some version of a national primary. Finally, because the caucus system itself is an alternative to the direct primary, one can legitimately ask how Iowa caucus-attenders compare with caucus-participants in other states. This permits us to begin addressing the question of how much Iowa caucus-attenders are unique because they are Iowans, and how much they are atypical because they are caucus-attenders.

Data Sources

The data available to address the questions implied above are in some cases fragmentary and the designs which generated them are not in every respect equivalent.[1] Briefly, the comparisons we make are based upon the following designs:

Caucus-Attenders. Mail surveys of caucus-attenders were taken in three states during the 1984 campaign: Iowa, Michigan and Virginia. Respondents in both parties were contacted as soon after the caucuses in their state as feasible. Larger samples of Democrats than Republicans were drawn since there was no nomination race òn the Republican side. Following the November elections, respondents to the spring survey were recontacted.[2] For purposes of this study, Iowa caucus-attenders will be compared with the Michigan and Virginia samples combined. No claim is made that Michigan and Virginia caucus participants together are representative of other caucus states. Most of the measures are taken from the spring questionnaire since it was more extensive than the post-election instrument. This means at times we compare measures from the caucus samples in the spring with indicators from other studies taken in the fall. Analysis of the items repeated on both waves of the caucus study reveal only very slight changes in the aggregate distributions.

Iowa General Electorate. A limited number of comparable items is available from an exit poll taken on election day in Iowa.[3]

National Election Study, 1984. A national sample of eligible voters interviewed immediately before and after the November election. For purposes of comparison with the caucus data, the "national electorate" is defined as all those eligible to vote in the NES sample, and partisan identifiers are those identifying with a party, including independents leaning toward a party.

Iowa State Convention Delegates. The culmination of the caucus process in Iowa is the state presidential nominating convention which meets in early June. One of its functions is to select the national convention delegates from Iowa. In 1984 we surveyed the Democratic state convention delegates at their June convention in Des Moines. The instrument was virtually identical to that employed in the caucus surveys. Delegates, like their counterparts throughout the study, were recontacted immediately following the November election.[4]

A Comparative Analysis
of Representation

A word is appropriate about how the analysis is presented. The first four comparison samples are taken from the Iowa electorate, the national electorate as a whole, identifiers with each party in the national electorate, and caucus attenders in the other two states studied. In each of these cases, the comparison assumes the relevant "constituency" of the Iowa caucus-attenders is the sample in question. Thus, for example, the comparison between Iowa caucus-attenders and caucus-attenders in other states is interesting from this perspective because Iowans are in some sense acting and standing for their counterparts in the other states. In negative terms, then, the question becomes, how unrepresentative of caucus attenders elsewhere are Iowans? A similar case could be made for Iowa voters, and for the national electorate.

The data are presented to facilitate a comparison of percentages. For example, the percent of Iowa caucus-attenders who graduated from college can be compared with the percentage of the constituency sample that graduated from college. A ratio of representation is also presented which provides the percentage of over or under representation (Lengle, 1981, p. 15). This is simply the percentage difference between Iowa caucus-attenders and the comparison sample divided by the percent in the comparison sample. Since 10 percent of Iowa caucus-attenders had 1983 family incomes in the $40,000–49,999 range and only 5 percent of Democrats in the Iowa electorate had incomes in this range, the five percent difference is apparent by comparing the percentage in each sample.[5] But since the caucus attenders were twice as likely to have incomes in that bracket, the index of overrepresentation is +100 percent. When Iowa caucus-attenders underrepresent the comparison group (as they do in the lowest income category when compared to Democrats in the Iowa electorate), the index takes on a negative value.

For the comparisons between Iowa Democratic caucus-attenders and the delegates to the Iowa State Democratic convention, the caucus-attenders become the "constituency" of state convention delegates. Thus, a positive index score indicates the delegates overrepresent a category of caucus-goers, and a negative score indicates delegates underrepresent the characteristic in question.

Demographic Comparisons

The first set of comparisons we present are on selected demographic variables across the relevant samples. The data are presented in Tables 2.1 (Democrats) and 2.2 (Republicans). In general, a pattern consistent with a "threshold" expectation emerges. That is, for education and income which are resources facilitating participation, Iowa caucus-attenders overrepresent higher status groups and underrepresent lower status categories in the Iowa and national electorates. On education, for example, Democratic caucus-attenders are more than twice as likely to have

26

TABLE 2.1   Selected Demographic Comparisons Across Samples of Democrats, 1984

	Iowa Caucus Attenders (%)	Iowa Exit Poll[a] (%)	National Electorate (%)	Identifier[b] (%)	Michigan and Virginia Caucus Attenders (%)	Iowa State Convention (N)
Education						
Less than HS Grad	11	9 (+22)	27 (-59)	26 (-58)	13 (-15)	4 (-64)
High School Grad	29	43 (-32)	36 (-19)	36 (-19)	18 (+61)	24 (-17)
Some College	23	30 (-23)	25 (-8)	24 (-4)	23 (0)	24 (+4)
College Grad	37	18 (+106)	17 (+118)	15 (+147)	47 (-21)	48 (+30)
N=	(1503)	(374)	(2243)	(776)	(2698)	(1276)
Family Income						
Under $20,000	36	54 (-33)	47 (-23)	52 (-31)	31 (+16)	29 (-19)
$20,000-29,999	25	20 (+25)	21 (+19)	21 (+19)	21 (+19)	25 (0)
$30,000-39,999	17	14 (+21)	14 (+21)	13 (+31)	18 (-6)	21 (+24)
$40,000-49,999	10	5 (+100)	8 (+25)	7 (+43)	13 (-23)	13 (+30)
$50,000 & over	11	5 (+120)	10 (+10)	7 (+57)	18 (-39)	11 (0)
N=	(1438)	(366)	(1990)	(953)	(2552)	(1220)
Race						
White	97	92 (+5)	87 (+11)	80 (+21)	75 (+29)	96 (-1)
Black	2	7 (-71)	11 (-82)	18 (-89)	22 (-90)	1 (-50)
Other	2	1 (+100)	2 (0)	2 (0)	3 (+1)	2 (0)
N=	(1506)	(375)	(2245)	(1065)	(2690)	(1281)
Age						
18-24	6	13 (-53)	13 (-54)	13 (-54)	7 (-14)	8 (+33)
25-29	8	14 (-42)	12 (+4)	12 (+4)	8 (0)	8 (0)
30-39	23	24 (-4)	25 (-8)	22 (+5)	23 (0)	33 (+43)
40-49	19	16 (+19)	15 (+29)	14 (+36)	19 (0)	20 (+5)
50-59	18	13 (+38)	12 (+50)	14 (+36)	18 (0)	18 (0)
60+	26	21 (+24)	24 (+8)	25 (+4)	25 (+4)	12 (-54)
N=	(1459)	(382)	(2237)	(1059)	(2580)	(1244)
Sex						
Male	48	45 (+7)	44 (+9)	42 (+14)	48 (0)	49 (+2)
Female	52	55 (-5)	56 (-7)	58 (-10)	52 (0)	51 (-2)
N=	(1493)	(353)	(2257)	(1070)	(2661)	(1291)
Religion						
Protestant	53	53 (0)	67 (-21)	63 (-16)	63 (-16)	51 (-4)
Catholic	33	30 (+10)	28 (+18)	31 (+06)	17 (+94)	32 (-3)
Jewish	1	0 (0)	3 (-66)	4 (-75)	3 (-66)	1 (0)
Other	13	17 (-24)	2 (+550)	3 (+333)	17 (-24)	16 (+19)
N=	(1480)	(376)	(2069)	(982)	(2627)	(1280)
Union Member	28	3 (-15)	22 (+7)	25 (+12)	33 (-15)	37 (+32)
N=	(1304)	(360)	(2249)	(1069)	(2311)	(1075)
Born Again?	24	13 (+85)	36 (-33)	36 (-33)	30 (-20)	20 (-17)
N=	(1499)	(380)	(1475)	(704)	(2615)	(1228)

[a]Source: ABC News Exit Poll.
[b]Source: *National Election Study*, 1984. Identifiers include independent-leaners.

TABLE 2.2   Selected Demographic Comparisons Across Samples of Republicans, 1984

	Iowa Caucus Attenders (%)	Iowa Exit Poll[a] (%)		Electorate (%)		National Identifier[b] (%)		Michigan and Virginia Caucus Attenders (%)	
Education									
Less than HS Graduate	6	77	(-14)	23	(-74)	17	(-65)	3	(+100)
High School Graduate	28	36	(-22)	36	(-22)	24	(-16)	13	(+115)
Some College	25	6	(+4)	25	(0)	28	(-11)	28	(-11)
College Graduate	41	31	(+32)	17	(+141)	21	(+95)	57	(-28)
N=	(641)	(397)		(2243)		(578)		(1048)	
Family Income									
Under $20,000	29	45	(-36)	47	(-38)	38	(-24)	14	(+107)
$20,000-29,999	20	18	(+11)	21	(-5)	22	(-9)	14	(+42)
$30,000-39,999	18	20	(-10)	14	(+29)	16	(+12)	21	(-14)
$40,000-49,999	13	7	(+86)	8	(+62)	9	(+44)	16	(-19)
$50,000 & over	20	9	(+122)	10	(+100)	16	(+25)	34	(-41)
N=	(592)	(385)		(1990)		(703)		(985)	
Race									
White	99	99	(0)	87	(+14)	97	(+2)	97	(-2)
Black	1	1	(0)	11	(-91)	1	(0)	2	(-50)
Other	--	--	(0)	2	(+2)	2	(+2)	2	(+2)
N=	(635)	(397)		(2245)		(579)		(1046)	
Age									
18-24	3	12	(-75)	13	(-77)	10	(-70)	6	(-50)
25-29	4	14	(-71)	12	(-67)	11	(-64)	5	(-20)
30-39	14	20	(-30)	25	(-36)	24	(-42)	19	(-26)
40-49	21	16	(+31)	15	(+40)	16	(+31)	20	(+5)
50-59	25	18	(+39)	12	(+108)	12	(+108)	26	(-4)
60+	32	20	(+60)	24	(+33)	27	(+19)	24	(+33)
N=	(621)	(400)		(2237)		(773)		(1006)	
Sex									
Male	55	50	(+10)	44	(+25)	45	(+22)	60	(-8)
Female	45	50	(-10)	56	(-20)	55	(-18)	40	(+12)
N=	(628)	(374)		(2257)		(780)		(1029)	
Religion									
Protestant	77	79	(-3)	67	(+15)	76	(+1)	72	(-17)
Catholic	12	12	(0)	28	(-57)	21	(-43)	20	(-40)
Jewish	0	0	(0)	3	(--)	1	(--)	1	(--)
Other	10	9	(+11)	2	(+400)	2	(+400)	8	(+25)
N=	(609)	(398)		(2069)		(738)		(1027)	
Union Member	18	11	(+64)	22	(-18)	17	(+6)	16	(+11)
N=	(539)	(382)		(2249)		(580)		(923)	
Born Again?	32	21	(+52)	36	(-11)	37	(-14)	30	(+6)
N=	(608)	(404)		(1475)		(589)		(1025)	

[a]Source: ABC News Exit Poll.
[b]Source: *National Election Study*, 1984. Identifiers include independent-leaners.

graduated from college than Democrats in the Iowa electorate. They are almost one and one-half times more likely to have a college education than Democrats in the national electorate. Likewise, Republican caucus-attenders are about one-third more likely to be well educated than Republicans in the Iowa electorate, and almost twice as likely as Republican identifiers nationally. A similar pattern obtains when income levels among Iowa caucus-attenders in both parties are compared with identifiers state- and nation-wide.

With respect to education and income comparisons with caucus-attenders in the other two states, Iowans appear to be more representative of identifiers in the national electorate. That is,· while there is a clear income and education bias among Iowans, caucus-goers in Michigan and Virginia are plainly more biased in this respect. Whereas Iowa Democratic caucus-attenders are about one and one-half times more likely to have graduated from college than Democratic identifiers in the electorate (37 vs. 15 percent respectively), Michigan and Virginia caucus-attenders are better than twice as likely than their copartisans nationally to be highly educated (47 vs. 15 percent). Hence, the index of representation shows Iowans under-representing the percentage of attenders in Michigan and Virginia with college degrees. Once again, this is a pattern which is fairly regular across other measures of political resources.

Rather than suppose that Michigan and Virginia caucus-attenders are from states with substantially larger proportions of well educated citizens, a better explanation is probably that one must cross a higher threshold in order to participate in those states. While there are some differences between what going to a caucus means in Iowa compared with the other states, probably the greatest difference is attributable to "campaign effects." The more visible, enduring, and proximate Iowa campaign doubtless generates a higher level of interest and information in that state than the relatively remote campaigns elsewhere. Hence, the Iowa caucus participant is "mobilized" by the political context in a way which is less characteristic of other caucus states.

Just in comparing education and income levels, then, the Iowa caucus-attenders can be said to overrepresent high-status characteristics when compared to their fellow partisans state- or nation-wide. Despite this clear status bias, the Iowans are more representative on such characteristics than caucus-participants in the two comparison states. The bias among Iowa caucus attenders is similar to that found in studies of primary voters and is probably attributable to the effort and commitment required to attend a precinct caucus on a cold evening in February. The bias is surely due less to the fact that these are Iowans, and more to the fact that they are unusually active politically. That the bias is weaker in Iowa than elsewhere, again, is not a reflection of Iowa being more

TABLE 2.3   Party and Candidate Support among Activist Samples, 1984

	Iowa Democrats	Republicans	Michigan and Virginia Democrats	Republicans	Iowa Delegates
Party Identification					
Strong	48%	62%	57%	76%	77%
Weak	27	24	17	11	12
Leaner	19	6	19	8	9
Independent	4	1	5	1	1
Opposite	2	6	2	4	--
N =	(1490)	(635)	(2676)	(1044)	(1317)
Mean Activity Scores					
Party Activity	.67	1.42	.85	2.37	1.93
General Campaign	.61	1.03	1.36	2.46	2.05
1984 General Election Candidate Support					
President	1.29	1.57	1.57	2.54	2.94
House	1.23	1.82	1.51	1.94	2.28
State and Local	1.39	1.80	1.20	1.87	2.53
Smallest N =	(873)	(395)	(1532)	(624)	(590)

typical than the other states. Rather, the relatively intense Iowa campaign mobilizes a less committed and more "typical" citizen than nomination campaigns elsewhere.

The comparisons in Tables 2.1 and 2.2 which do not involve variables directly related to social status will not detain us, although there are some interesting findings. For example, the Democrats in Iowa may have slightly under-mobilized union members to their caucuses, and born-again Christians in both parties appear to be overrepresented. Also, consistent with other research on political participation, the age bias in favor of older cohorts is quite clearly present among caucus attenders.

Partisan Support

The vitally partisan process of selecting a presidential nominee should attract participants strongly committed to their party. As the data in Table 2.3 demonstrate, caucus-attenders are strongly identified with their party. With respect to party identification, Iowa caucus-attenders are less strongly identified than their counterparts in Michigan and Virginia, and Democrats, regardless of state, are less strongly identified than

Republicans. This pattern is reinforced by the "activity scores" which measure the mean number of activities respondents engaged in for their party and in past campaigns.[6] Likewise, the measures of 1984 general election candidate support show higher levels of activity by Republicans than by Democrats, and less activity by Iowans than by those in Michigan and Virginia. Interestingly, Democratic state convention delegates most closely resemble Republican caucus-participants in the comparison states in their partisan support and activity levels.

These data, even more clearly than those in Tables 2.1 and 2.2, support the idea that Iowans face a lower participation threshold than those in other states. The intensity of the campaign in Iowa is what is most clearly different about the state's process. The fact that Republicans uniformly emerge as more active and supportive of their party is again almost surely due to the context of 1984. Without a nomination fight in their party, a higher degree of commitment was necessary to motivate participation. That Iowa Republicans appear to be slightly less active and supportive than their copartisans elsewhere may be due to the fact that the Democratic nomination campaign spilled over to generate interest on the GOP side.

Once again, the point should be clear. It is not that Iowans are by nature less partisan or less active. Indeed, were the Virginia or Washington or Colorado caucuses first, one can imagine the limelight would shift away from Iowa, and the average caucus-attender there would be quite similar to the other states. By being first, by attracting so much candidate and media attention, the Iowa caucuses actually become more representative of their party's rank and file than they would otherwise be. That appears to be the case, at least, insofar as the comparisons on basic status and partisan commitment measures is concerned.

Ideology and Issues

If the data hold true to similar studies in the past, we can expect activists to differ from the popular bases of their parties in ways consistent with the demographic and party support differences we have already seen. A number of studies have found that activists tend to have more firmly held ideological and issue positions than do partisans in the public (McClosky et al., 1960; Kirkpatrick, 1975; Jackson et al., 1982; Miller and Jennings, 1986). This disturbs some analysts concerned about representation since activists, whether they are caucus-attenders or national convention delegates, may pursue their own ideological interests in making party policy and supporting a presidential nominee, rather than anticipate the interests of the broader electorate. In some respects, then, the question of how well activists reflect ideological and issue

TABLE 2.4   Selected Demographic Comparisons Across Samples of Democrats, 1984

	Iowa Caucus Attenders (%)	Iowa Exit Poll (%)	National Electorate (%)	Identifier (%)	Michigan and Virginia Caucus Attenders (%)	Iowa State Convention (N)
Ideological						
Extremely Liberal	6		2 (+200)	4 (+50)	9 (-33)	11 (+67)
Liberal	31	30 (+103)	10 (+21)	17 (+82)	39 (-21)	43 (+26)
Slightly Liberal	24		13 (+85)	20 (+20)	20 (+20)	20 (-17)
Moderate	23	43 (-47)	33 (-30)	38 (-39)	18 (+28)	15 (-30)
Slightly Conservative	11		20 (-45)	13 (-15)	9 (+22)	7 (-36)
Conservative	5	28 (-39)	18 (-72)	8 (-38)	6 (-16)	4 (-20)
Extremely Conservative	1		2 (-100)	1 (0)	0 --	0 --
N =	(1383)	(371)	(1555)	(722)	(2502)	(1278)
Aid to Central America						
Favor	11		25 (-56)	20 (-45)	16 (-31)	6 (-45)
---	13		20 (-35)	17 (-23)	14 (-7)	8 (-38)
Oppose	77		55 (+40)	63 (+22)	71 (+8)	86 (+12)
N =	(1412)		(1696)	(813)	(2541)	(1249)
Increased Defense Spending						
Favor	8		36 (-72)	26 (-69)	11 (-27)	6 (-25)
---	4		32 (-88)	29 (-88)	5 (-20)	1 (-75)
Oppose	86		32 (+169)	45 (+91)	84 (+2)	93 (+8)
N =	(1460)		(1933)	(905)	(2604)	(1271)
Government Medical Insurance						
Favor	61		38 (+61)	45 (+36)	70 (-13)	70 (+15)
---	18		21 (-14)	20 (-10)	14 (+29)	14 (-22)
Oppose	21		42 (-50)	35 (-40)	16 (+31)	16 (-24)
N =	(1453)		(792)	(306)	(2615)	(1270)

preferences of the relevant comparison group goes to the heart of analyses of representation.

Comparative data on a 7-point ideology scale and on three issues for which comparable measures exist are presented in Tables 2.4 and 2.5. Particularly on the ideology scale among Democrats, the comparisons fit the expected pattern. Democratic caucus-attenders in Iowa are about twice as likely to opt for the "liberal" label as Democrats in the Iowa electorate.[7] Caucus-attenders were noticeably less likely to identify themselves as moderate or conservative. A very similar pattern exists among Democrats when the Iowa caucus-participants are compared with identifiers in the national electorate. Once again, the difference is magnified among state convention delegates. In the Iowa electorate, only 30 percent of Democrats think of themselves as liberal, the proportion liberal jumps to 61 percent among caucus-attenders, and reaches 74 percent among state convention delegates.

Curiously, the Republican identifiers are considerably closer to their partisan affiliates in the Iowa electorate than the Democrats are to theirs. The Republicans underrepresent moderates, but their overrepresentation of conservatives is relatively slight. When compared with the less

TABLE 2.5   Ideological and Issue Comparisons among Republicans, 1984

	Iowa Caucus Attenders (%)	Iowa Exit Poll (%)	National Electorate (%)	National Identifier (%)	Michigan and Virginia Caucus Attenders (%)
Ideology					
Extremely Liberal	1		2 (-50)	-- --	-- --
Liberal	4	7 (+43)	10 (-60)	4 (0)	2 (+100)
Slightly Liberal	5		13 (-62)	7 (-28)	3 (+67)
Moderate	15	24 (-38)	33 (-55)	25 (-40)	7 (+114)
Slightly Conservative	26		20 (+30)	29 (-10)	20 (+3)
Conservative	43	68 (+10)	18 (+139)	31 (+39)	56 (-23)
Extremely Conservative	6		2 (+200)	4 (+50)	12 (-50)
N =	(630)	(385)	(1555)	(682)	(1039)
Aid to Central America					
Favor	42		25 (+68)	32 (+31)	70 (-39)
---	21		20 (+5)	24 (-12)	14 (+50)
Oppose	37		55 (-33)	43 (-19)	16 (+131)
N =	(610)		(1096)	(681)	(1016)
Increased Defense Spending					
Favor	42		36 (+17)	47 (-11)	72 (-42)
---	9		32 (-72)	36 (-69)	5 (+80)
Oppose	49		32 (+53)	18 (+172)	23 (+113)
N =	(629)		(1933)	(802)	(1034)
Government Health Insurance					
Favor	24		38 (-37)	28 (-14)	17 (+41)
---	12		21 (-43)	21 (-43)	11 (+9)
Oppose	64		42 (+52)	50 (+28)	71 (-10)
N =	(627)		(792)	(341)	(1033)

conservative identifiers nationally, the overrepresentation is a bit greater. The differences between Democrats and Republicans on this score are due to the greater homogeneity of the Republican party on the ideology scale at both activist and mass levels.

On the issues, Iowa Democratic caucus attenders were more likely than all comparison groups save delegates to favor aid to Central America, and to oppose increased defense spending. Caucus-attenders favor national health insurance more than Democrats nationwide, though they are less supportive than delegates in their state or caucus-participants in the other two states.[8]

Republicans in Iowa were dramatically more likely to oppose increases in defense spending than were Republicans nationally or in the two comparison states. On both aid to Central America and government health insurance, the Iowa Republicans also appear to be more liberal than caucus-goers elsewhere.

Activists' Ideological Perceptions

The question of how activists perceive others' ideological preferences is important both in its own right and because of its potential impact on what activists do when they participate. It is also a topic which deserves a much more detailed analysis than can be offered here. A discussion of representation, however, must broach the subject since the quality and impact of these perceptions may affect participants' ability to "act for" others.

Figure 2.1 presents both the self-identified location of NES respondents, and respondents to the caucus surveys. The seven-point scale employed in both studies was identical. In addition, activists' perceptions of the national electorate, of the two parties, and of the major candidates are presented.

The conventional wisdom that the general electorate is relatively centrist, and that the two parties have centers of gravity somewhat to the left and right is supported in these results. It is also the case that Democratic caucus-attenders are further to the left than identifiers in the electorate. As we saw in Table 2.4, participants in the Iowa caucuses are closer to identifiers in the national electorate than are caucus-attenders elsewhere. Similarly, Republicans attending in Iowa are less extreme on average than their counterparts in the comparison states, although they are to the right of Republican identifiers in the electorate.

When activists survey the ideological landscape, they do not see things the same way. There is greatest consistency in perceptions of the electorate as a whole. On that question, the different activist samples agree in perceiving the electorate as close to the center of the scale. And, taking the NES data as an appropriate referent, the activists' perceptions are close to the mark. A partisan bias is clearly evident in the data on perception of parties and candidates. Democrats perceive the Republican party and Ronald Reagan as further to the right than Republicans do. Republicans see the Democratic party and the three Democratic candidates as further to the left than do the Democrats. This pattern may result from a tendency to "push away" the opposite party in order to maintain cognitive balance, or it may reflect a need among partisans to see their own candidates and party as more moderate, or both.[9]

Despite this partisan difference, there is remarkable consistency across the samples. All activist samples agree that Ronald Reagan is to the right of the Republican party and that George Bush is more moderate than his mentor. All see the average American as about in the center, and Gary Hart as the most conservative of the Democratic candidates shown. Jesse Jackson is uniformly seen as the most liberal candidate. One break in the order across the five samples is when Walter Mondale and the Democratic party are compared. Iowa caucus-participants in both parties see them as at virtually the same spot on the scale. Michigan and Virginia respondents see the nominee and his party as being extremely

Figure 2.1
Ideological Patterns Among Activists and the Mass Public: 1984

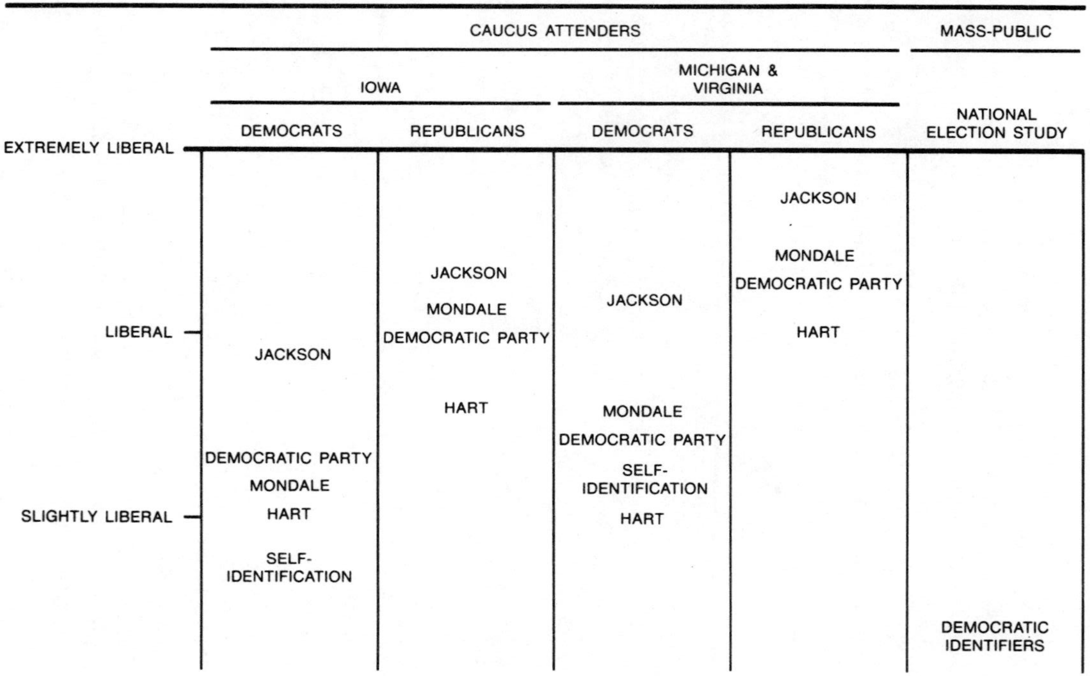

	CAUCUS ATTENDERS				MASS-PUBLIC
	IOWA		MICHIGAN & VIRGINIA		
	DEMOCRATS	REPUBLICANS	DEMOCRATS	REPUBLICANS	NATIONAL ELECTION STUDY
EXTREMELY LIBERAL					
	JACKSON	JACKSON MONDALE DEMOCRATIC PARTY	JACKSON	JACKSON MONDALE DEMOCRATIC PARTY	
LIBERAL		HART	MONDALE DEMOCRATIC PARTY SELF-IDENTIFICATION HART	HART	
	DEMOCRATIC PARTY MONDALE HART SELF-IDENTIFICATION				
SLIGHTLY LIBERAL					DEMOCRATIC IDENTIFIERS

AMERICAN VOTER — REPUBLICAN IDENTIFIERS — (682)

AMERICAN VOTER — BUSH — REPUBLICAN PARTY — SELF-IDENTIFICATION — REAGAN — (975)

AMERICAN VOTER — BUSH — REPUBLICAN PARTY — REAGAN — (2296)

AMERICAN VOTER — BUSH — SELF-IDENTIFICATION — REPUBLICAN PARTY — REAGAN — (557)

AMERICAN VOTER — REPUBLICAN PARTY — BUSH — REAGAN — (1259)

MIDDLE-OF-THE-ROAD

SLIGHTLY CONSERVATIVE

CONSERVATIVE

EXTREMELY CONSERVATIVE

SMALLEST N

close, but place Mondale to the left of the party. The only other discrepancy is the Iowa Democrats' placement of Bush slightly to the right of the Republican party.

This mapping of the ideological space in 1984 was widely shared. It conforms to the conventional view that the public is in the center, and that "the parties" (the referent is admittedly vague) are distinctly off-center. It suggests, to the extent that simple spatial models can capture a significant part the strategic problem faced by candidates (Downs, 1957; Aldrich, 1980), the two stages of the presidential selection process establish a fundamental tension. Nomination candidates must appeal to primary voters, caucus-attenders, convention delegates, and other activists who are markedly to the left or right of the general electorate which must be wooed if the White House is to be won (Aronson and Ordeshook, 1972). This is but another example of the general problem posed by this paper: How representative are Iowa caucus-attenders? (Caucus-attenders generally? Convention delegates? Primary voters?) Nomination activists of any stripe do not reflect the general electorate. What's more, Figure 2.1 makes clear that the activists included in this study are fully aware that they are not ideologically typical of the American electorate. Thus, candidates are faced with first satisfying an atypical sector of the population in order to compete against the opposition in the general election. That appears to be an inescapable feature of contemporary presidential politics.

Analysis of Candidate Support

Knowing something about who nomination participants support is at the core of the question of representation. If participants systematically support candidates not preferred by the supposed constituency, a significant breakdown in the process could be presumed. By the same token, if participants' candidate preferences and support behavior reflects those characteristics which distinguish participants from nonparticipants, a bias may result. Thus, for example, if caucus-attenders choose candidates based upon their own ideological preferences, the kinds of candidates selected would probably not reflect the ideological interests of the general electorate. This follows from the fact that caucus-attenders are, both in reality and by their own description, different from the electorate.

Table 2.6 presents the 1984 nomination candidate preferences of the activist samples, along with their mean levels of candidate support activity, and their levels of exposure to the major nomination campaigns.[10] The candidate preference measures in particular are doubtless sensitive to time factors as the 1984 campaign proceeded (Bartels, 1985; 1987), a fact which makes the comparisons in the table somewhat problematic.[11]

TABLE 2.6   Candidate Support and Campaign Exposure among Democratic Activists, 1984

	Caucus Attenders		
	Iowa %	Michigan and Virginia %	Iowa State Delegates %
First Choice			
Walter Mondale	41	48	47
Gary Hart	32	26	29
Jesse Jackson	3	17	3
Alan Cranston	5	2	7
John Glenn	4	4	3
George McGovern	15	6	12
Smallest N =	(1291)	(2218)	(1138)
Mondale/Hart Preference			
Mondale	51	62	55
Hart	49	38	45
Smallest N =	(1324)	(2281)	(1155)
Nomination Candidate Support Scores			
Mondale	1.23	1.36	2.25
Hart	.59	.48	1.33
Jackson	.04	.35	.13
Smallest N =	(837)	(1532)	(590)
Nomination Campaign Exposure Scores			
Mondale	2.79	2.03	3.65
Hart	2.21	1.65	3.10
Jackson	.96	1.37	1.30
Smallest N =	(1490)	(2676)	(1317)

It is clear, for whatever reason, that caucus-goers in Iowa were more supportive of the Hart campaign than were those in the other states. By the same token, it is no surprise that both the Mondale and Hart campaigns generated a higher average level of exposure in Iowa than in Michigan and Virginia. Jesse Jackson's campaign was more active in the comparison states than in Iowa.

Explaining Candidate Support among Caucus-Participants

Candidate support in the nomination stage is not as well understood among scholars as is voting choice in the general election. In part, this is due to the absence of partisanship as a powerful structuring cue to participants. Nomination campaigns are, after all, contests within the party, not between the parties. Of perhaps greater importance is the complexity of nomination races. They are strung out in time and over a number of different kinds of contests in different states. Often they involve several candidates. And, because the result of the nomination contest is the choice of someone to run in the general election, the choice is not final. Participants may (or may not) look ahead to the general election stage in selecting from among contenders in the nomination race. Likewise, of course, candidates must first win the nomination to be able to compete credibly for the White House. Their strategies and appeals are doubtless a mix of those based upon the personal preferences of participants and stimulating an interest in seizing or retaining the presidency against the opposition in the fall.

We include in the analysis of candidate support a set of demographic variables which reflect the possibility that candidates may target their appeals to segments of the party. Moreover, as we have seen, demography distinguishes to some extent participants from nonparticipants.

Attitudinal and perceptual variables are also likely to be important. Indeed, for a host of reasons, they are almost certain to be most powerful statistically. Unfortunately, the inferences one can safely draw from such results are more difficult to untangle. Strength of party identification is included to capture long-term support of the party. Ideological proximity to the candidates taps a large part of the issue-based affinity activists have for candidates (Stone, 1982; Abramowitz and Stone, 1984). Perceptions of how closely candidates represent broader voter and party ideological sentiment measures part of the tension candidates face between these two forces in the process. Perhaps more important are perceptions of the candidates' chances in the nomination and general election campaigns. Estimates of chances in the nomination campaign are likely to affect support because participants want to choose from among the most viable candidates, and because momentum and bandwagon effects appear to influence candidate choice (Bartels, 1985; 1987). A candidate's chances against the opposition party in the fall is relevant because participants have an interest in supporting a candidate capable of beating the opposition, even when that candidate is not the most reflective of issue or ideological concerns in the field (see Coleman, 1972). Finally, since campaigns are designed to influence supporters, we include a measure of campaign exposure.

With one important exception, we do not consider the complex relationships among these variables. Doubtless something like a causal chain could be constructed from demographic characteristics through perceptions and attitudes. For example, if "yuppies" were inclined to support Gary Hart on grounds linked to demography, a full explanation would recognize that those characteristics might have had powerful effects on how closely Hart was perceived to reflect ideological preferences, his chances in the nomination race, his electability, and so on. Doubtless,

TABLE 2.7   Predictors of Hart-Mondale Relative Support among Democratic Caucus Attenders, 1984

| | Relative Ranking | | | | Relative Support Activity | | | |
| | Equation 1 | | Equation 2 | | Equation 1 | | Equation 2 | |
	b	Beta	b	Beta	b	Beta	b	Beta
Demographics								
Education	-.050	-.020	-.038	-.019	.059	.036	.049	.029
Age	-.048*	-.031	-.015	-.010	-.069*	-.053	-.045	-.036
Black	-.354*	-.041	-.282	-.032	.190	.025	.135	.017
Income	-.027	-.020	-.034	-.025	-.027	-.023	-.029	-.026
Union Member	.110	.016	.090	.013	-.222	-.038	-.178	-.030
Union Leader	-.413*	-.054	-.241	-.038	-.766*	-.119	-.687*	-.116
Iowa	.098	.019	.066	.012	-.015	-.003	.012	.003
Party Support								
Strength of Party Id.	.368*	.157	.272*	.117	.136*	.068	.098	.049
Campaign Exposure	.325*	.165	.207*	.105	.425*	.263	.390*	.240
Attitudes and Perceptions								
Ideological Proximity	.341*	.194	.229*	.130	.153*	.091	.107*	.063
Proximity to American Voters	-.095*	-.047	-.084*	-.042	-.007	-.004	-.004	-.002
Proximity to Democratic Party	.071*	.041	-.003	-.002	.052	.030	.037	.021
Nomination Chances	.013*	.136	.009*	.100	.006*	.077	.004	.048
Electability	.041*	.352	.025*	.216	.026*	.264	.020*	.206
Candidate Evaluation			.761*	.406			.300*	.182
R²	.413		.523		.286		.308	
N =	(1833)		(1533)		(1128)		(1109)	

Note: *P < .05

too, respondents were more likely to remember mail contact from a campaign to which they were favorably disposed, and personal contact with a candidate is likely to be under the control of the respondent as much as it reflect candidate behavior.[12] Because of their complexity, we defer an in-depth treatment of these issues.

The measures of candidate support are two: candidate rankings, and support behavior on behalf of the candidate. In Table 2.7 we report analyses of relative support of Hart vs. Mondale. The dependent variable is simply the relative ranking or the relative level of activity offered in support of the candidate. A negative score indicates greater support for Mondale than for Hart, a positive score indicates greater support for Hart. These are regressed on the demographic, attitudinal, perceptual and campaign exposure indicators described above.[13] A separate analysis of support for Jesse Jackson is presented below.

Consider the "Equation 1" results first. The demographics provide almost no independent explanation of candidate support either for relative ranking of Hart and Mondale, or for actual campaign activity. Race achieves statistical significance in explaining relative ranking, and age has an effect on activity levels, but the effects are weak. That blacks were more supportive of Mondale conforms to the conventional wisdom about 1984, but the weak age effect is contrary to the perception that Hart appealed more to the young. The one variable with a consistent effect across the two dependent measures is union leadership. Dummy variables capturing union membership and leadership were entered to assess the impact of the endorsement Mondale received from organized labor. This, and more detailed analysis reported elsewhere (Rapoport, Abramowitz and Stone, 1986), suggests that members were not significantly different from non-union members in their candidate support. But union "leaders"[14] were significantly more likely to rank Mondale ahead of Hart, and to back up this preference with higher levels of activity.

That strength of party identification is associated with increased Hart support also conforms to conventional understandings of the 1984 contest. Hart presented himself as a candidate not tied to the traditional trappings of the Democratic party. In some respects his was an insurgent candidacy. Once he had "succeeded" in Iowa and won in New Hampshire, moreover, he was the principal alternative to Walter Mondale for many Democrats. Given Mondale's role in the party prior to the election, it is no surprise that weaker identifiers were those most likely to be searching for another candidate.

Among the "attitudes and perceptions" set of explanatory variables, the one modest surprise is that proximity to the average American voter actually has a significant negative effect on candidate ranking (the zero-order correlation is precisely 0). Both proximity to the electorate and to the Democratic party are variables which more likely explain perceptions of nomination and general election chances.[15]

As we have already seen, activists' ideological preferences have a significant effect on nomination candidate support. This, then, is a potential source of bias in the process. At the same time, however, the noticeably stronger effect of electability may offset the bias. That is, nomination participants face a decision problem which can be understood as a tradeoff between their own personal preferences (ideological proximity to the candidates) and their perceptions of what will be acceptable to the general electorate in the fall campaign (candidate electability). We have seen that activists understand their ideological preferences are markedly different from the norm in the electorate. Therefore, they cannot escape the problem by supposing their preferences are shared by the electorate and amount to a reasonable strategy for nomination and general election success. These results indicate that participants are on the whole more influenced by electability than by their ideological preferences, and less affected by nomination than by general election chances. They square with earlier work on 1980 which show a tendency of activists to balance their personal preferences with their desire to support a winner, and that the latter interest outweighs the former (Stone and Abramowitz, 1983; Abramowitz and Stone, 1984).

One of the major problems in interpreting these results remains unaddressed in the Equation 1 results. Judgments about candidate chances, perceptions of ideological proximity, and campaign exposure measures may arguably result as much from candidate evaluations as they independently drive the candidate support measures. That is, liking Mondale more than Hart may easily generate a favorable perception of Mondale's chances. Especially in 1984 when Hart and Mondale failed to distinguish themselves sharply in their ideological positions, the perceived differences between them could also result from rationalizations of positive affect. And the campaign exposure measures, while designed to tap the effect of the campaign on the individual, doubtless are contaminated by a selection bias resulting from attraction to the candidates.

Disentangling these confounding effects, and especially estimating the reciprocal effects of the variables on one another is a daunting task well beyond the bounds of this paper. However, the results reported as Equation 2 are designed to speak to the issue in a fundamental way. Equation 2 is identical to Equation 1 except that it includes a measure of candidate affect.[16] A positive evaluation of a candidate is conceptually distinct from support for the candidate because other considerations such as electability or ideological proximity should have an independent effect. Participants often choose to support a candidate other than the one whom they evaluate most positively. But candidate evaluation is itself a "proximate cause" of candidate support. Many of the variables which affect candidate support doubtless have an effect on evaluation. Equation 2 ignores these effects, and presents the Equation 1 effects independent of candidate affect. Presumably, then, the campaign exposure, ideological proximity, nomination chances and electability effects reported in these results are uncontaminated by rationalizations of candidate evaluation.[17]

The results in Table 2.7 which include candidate evaluation are reassuring to the interpretations offered above. Note especially that campaign exposure, ideological proximity, and electability remain strong and statistically significant. These effects cannot be understood as mere rationalizations of attraction to the candidates. Contact with participants through campaign matters. Calculations of ideological proximity are independent of candidate attractiveness, and have an impact on support. And participants assess competing candidates' chances against the opposition party in the general election, and are quite powerfully influenced by those judgments.

These results appear to make very good sense. Nomination activists do care about the issues, and they do not act solely because they want to help their party. But they are dependent upon the party to help produce policy which they favor. Thus, while motivated by policy concerns, they must also consider what will "fly" in the general election campaign. After all, for a Democratic activist, almost any Democratic candidate is preferable to almost any Republican. This is why electability has such a strong effect.

Nomination chances are understandably less important, especially when the choice is framed between two competing candidates. To be sure, nomination chances are relevant early in the campaign when participants seek to avoid wasting their efforts on a candidate who will not survive the process. But when the choice is narrowed, the interest in basing one's choice in part on anticipation of the fall campaign is compelling. As James Coleman (1972, p. 334) put it:

> Party electorates are not merely expressive voters, electing that candidate as their nominee whom they themselves find most appealing. Instead, they elect a candidate with some view toward the final election. If their interest is in maximizing their gains in the main election, they would certainly not be doing so if they nominated . . . [a] candidate who had no chance of election, no matter how fully he satisfied their tastes.

The Case of Jesse Jackson

The Jackson candidacy in 1984 was unique in several respects. Jackson was the first contemporary black candidate for a major party nomination to gain national credibility and have a substantial impact on the campaign. His candidacy was insurgent in that it threatened the mainstream Mondale effort. But unlike Hart's campaign, Jackson did not depend for his support on offering a credible alternative to Mondale. As Table 2.8 shows, Jackson support was most powerfully influenced by race. "Strategic" factors like nomination and general election chances are much weaker than in the Mondale-Hart comparisons, or they are absent altogether. Indeed, in Jackson's case, the basis of his support was more strongly ideological than it was based upon wanting to back a winner. Campaign effects are also suspect (they do not reach statistical significance when candidate evaluation is included). And it is no surprise that the weaker the partisanship, the more likely nomination activists were to support Jackson.

These results, again, make sense. Jackson's candidacy was based heavily on a moral appeal, a call to action by the dispossessed in the Democratic

TABLE 2.8   Predictors of Jesse Jackson Rankings among Caucus Attenders, 1984

	Equation 1		Equation 2	
	b	Beta	b	Beta
Demographics				
Education	-.062	-.035	-.104*	-.060
Age	-.114*	-.083	-.088*	-.064
Black	2.179*	.381	1.880*	.330
Income	-.024	-.019	-.025	-.020
Union Member	-.015	-.002	.048	.008
Union Leader	.141	.019	.131	.018
Iowa	.165	.036	.110	.025
Party Support				
Strength of Party Id.	.109*	.051	.110*	.052
Campaign Exposure	.110*	.066	.066	.040
Attitudes and Perceptions				
Ideological Proximity	.398*	.216	.240*	.132
Proximity to American Voters	-.138*	-.073	-.044	-.023
Proximity to Democratic Party	.053	.024	-.003	-.001
Nomination Chances	.008	.068	.006*	.052
Electability	.020*	.172	.011*	.091
Candidate Evaluation			.774*	.392
R²		.363		.486
N =		(1027)	(1006)	

Note: *P < .05

party. It was predicated upon mobilizing into the party those who had not participated, especially blacks. It was an attempt to transform the party and therefore American politics, but its credibility did not depend upon a realistic claim to winning the nomination or the White House. Whether Jackson will have the impact on American politics he seeks remains to be seen. But his support in 1984 was clearly responsive to his call.

Conclusions

We have suggested the results of the analysis of candidate support make sense. Nomination participants become active and offer their support because they are committed to a set of policy goals broadly consistent with that of their party. They find the party a congenial place to pursue their political interests because of this broadly shared perspective. Hence, on the whole, they are strongly identified with and active in the party. Of course, parties embrace many factions and are sometimes torn by bitter conflict. Nomination campaigns institutionalize this conflict, and even exploit it. In choosing between and among the candidates, participants must decide how to balance competing interests. Their interest in backing a winner may conflict with their personal evaluations of candidate quality or with their ideological goals. But given that they are in some sense committed to their party, by helping it win they also further their ideological and policy objectives.

If these results make sense from the perspective of understanding why nomination participants become active and choose to support a candidate, what are their implications for the question of representation? They are not entirely reassuring. Caucus-attenders and other nomination activists are not typical of the larger populations they may be presumed to "act for." They are better educated, older, and have higher incomes. They are more committed to and active in their party than the average citizen. They are less likely to be indifferent on the issues, and are more "extreme" in their ideological commitments. These ideological preferences do have an impact on their candidate support which may result in candidates facing a tension between their nomination supporters and those they must satisfy in the general electorate.

The distortion introduced by the influence of ideological proximity on nomination activists' candidate support may be minimal if one thinks of the relevant constituency of nomination participants as party identifiers in the national electorate. Moreover, a case can be made that forces such as the nomination campaigns which push candidates out from the center are a desirable feature of electoral politics (Page, 1978). Assessing the implications of these results is further complicated by the fact that activists appear not to be influenced by perceptions of candidate proximity to the average American voter or to the Democratic party. Perhaps activists are aware that ideology plays a limited role in general election politics and that other factors such as the ability of candidates to project well on television are far more important in explaining electability (Abramowitz, Rapoport and Stone, 1985). And of course, we have argued the fact that candidate electability is a more potent explanation of candidate support than ideology further softens the potential for distortion.

What of Iowa? Certainly it is true that the Iowa caucus-attenders have a significant and disproportionate impact on the nomination process. But what does this mean? Any sequential process would endow upon those who start a similar status. The research reported here suggests that the nature of the campaign in Iowa (or, most probably, anyplace designated as first) moderates the atypical features of the activist population. If caucus-attenders generally are higher status, more committed to their party, and more ideological than the average citizen, the Iowa caucus-attender is less so. The circumstantial evidence is strong that Iowa caucus-attenders better represent the broader electorate on these dimensions not because Iowa is a good bellweather state, but simply because of the political context that results from going first.

Is this to say all concerns about representativeness can be laid to rest? One guesses not. The lack of formal accountability mechanisms in the process colors any assessment, as do perceptions of the alternatives. Primary voters, even in the large, heterogeneous states, are not representative. Caucus-attenders are not representative. Convention delegates are not representative. A fuller assessment of the process demands better evidence than we now have on how these different strata in the parties decide whom to support. We also require a fuller understanding of the winnowing that goes on through the protracted campaign. Indeed, the Iowa caucuses in 1988 endorsed candidates in both parties (Gephardt on the Democratic side, and Dole in the Republican race) which did not impress voters in later primaries. Certainly it can be said that "momentum" generated by early contests like Iowa is not the final word.

Research is proceeding on these fronts, and there is reason to hope substantial improvements in our understanding will shortly result. At the same time, it is probably not too far-fetched to say that serious questions about the presidential nomination process will continue to be raised, and debates over reforms and counter-reforms will be prominent for the foreseeable future.

Notes

We are grateful to the National Science Foundation for the support to carry out the caucus-attender and state convention surveys (SES-8308871), to the National Election Study for the 1984 national survey data, and to ABC News for the Iowa exit poll data. Jay McCann, David Davis, and Eric Bryant provided valuable research assistance. The Institute of Behavioral Science at the University of Colorado provided Stone with time off from teaching and Jean Umbreit helped with the preparation of the manuscript.

1. We do not discuss all of the technical differences in the designs. We have selected variables from each study employed which are as equivalent as possible, and we have avoided comparisons where the question format was substantially different, even if the item involved the same general issue. Complete accounts of question wording for all items employed in this study are available from the authors on request.

2. The response to the nomination survey averaged 45 percent among Democrats in the three states, and 50 percent among Republicans. It varied

from a low of 35 percent among Michigan Democrats to a high of 60 percent
from Virginia Republicans. Response to the post-election wave averaged just
under 70 percent of those returning the first round questionnaire.

3. We are grateful to Douglas Muzzio of ABC News for providing the data.
The sample was designed to be representative of the Iowa electorate and was
taken as part of a national sample.

4. Delegates were surveyed at the convention during the proceedings by
placing questionnaires on all seats. The response rate to the first wave was 55
percent. Of these, 44.5 percent responded to the second wave mailing.

5. This is a good time to point out that the one variable employed which
is not strictly equivalent across samples is income. For all samples but the exit
poll data, the question asked for 1983 family income. The exit poll did not
specify the year in the question: "Before taxes your annual household income
is . . ." Thus the income comparisons involving the exit poll data probably
understate the differences to some degree.

6. The party index counts the number of party positions held at any time
in the past by respondents. The offices on a list of nine vary from member of
a local party committee to elected office to delegate to a national convention.
The campaign activity index counts the number of campaigns the respondent
was "very active" in during the past 5 years. The list of campaigns covers seven
levels from the presidency to "local offices."

7. The Iowa exit poll did not offer a 7-point scale to respondents. Instead,
the question posed three alternatives: "liberal," "moderate," and "conservative."
For purposes of comparison with the exit poll data, then, we have simply
aggregated the 7-point item employed in the caucus survey.

8. The issue items put to exit poll respondents were simply not comparable
to those asked in the other studies.

9. A second source of bias evident is the activist's own opinion. That is,
respondents may associate their party and candidates' positions with their own,
and tend to view the opposite party's as contrary to their own views. Among
activists, the correlations are not strong. Democratic and Republican caucus
participants' own ideological positions correlate almost not at all with their
perceptions of the average American voter ($-.05$ and $.06$ respectively). Democratic
perceptions of their party's major contenders show a weak positive correlation
with respondents' own positions (averaging $.17$) and a stronger negative association with their perceptions of Reagan's ideology ($-.30$). Republicans' own
positions correlate negatively with their perceptions of Democratic candidates'
positions (averaging $-.27$) and are uncorrelated with their understanding of
Reagan's views ($.03$).

10. The "first choice" percentages in the table reflect the proportions of each
sample ranking that candidate first among the complete list. The "Mondale/
Hart" preferences result from a comparison of the Mondale and Hart rankings
of each respondent. Thus the proportion preferring Mondale to Hart is the
percentage who ranked the Minnesotan ahead of Senator Hart, even if neither
candidate was ranked first. The nomination support scores are mean counts of
the number of activities in support of a candidate during the nomination campaign.

The activities listed were six and included such things as contributing money, canvassing, and clerical work for the campaign. Exposure scores are also counts of six items tapping exposure to the candidate's nomination campaign. They included such items as meeting the candidate personally, receiving mail or some other contact from the campaign, and exposure to media advertising.

11. The Iowa questionnaires were mailed in March, the other two states were about a month later in getting out, and the delegate questionnaires were distributed in June.

12. Although Iowans were almost exactly twice as likely to report having met Mondale or Hart personally as were respondents in the other two states. Presumably that says more about the campaigns than it does about the relative dedication of Iowans to these two candidates.

13. The attitudinal, perceptual and campaign exposure variables are all scored in a manner equivalent to the dependent variables. Thus, for example, "ideological proximity" is really relative proximity to Hart and Mondale. A negative score indicates closer proximity to Mondale, a positive score indicates the respondent is closer to Hart. A similar coding is used for relative proximity to the average American voter, nomination chances, electability, campaign exposure, and candidate evaluation.

14. Those in our survey who indicated they occupied positions of leadership in a labor union or who said they were "active members" of the union.

15. The zero-order correlations are weak, but detectable. For an analysis focusing on explaining perceptions of candidate chances, see Abramowitz, Rapoport, and Stone (1985), and Abramowitz and Stone (1984).

16. After asking respondents to evaluate candidates on a number of specific candidate traits, we requested an overall evaluation. Responses were ordered on a five-point scale from "outstanding" to "poor." Again, the indicator employed here is a relative measure of Mondale-Hart evaluations.

17. Much as the results from Equation 1 overstate the effects because they fail to take into account the reciprocal consequences of candidate evaluation, Equation 2 understates the effect of these variables because it ignores their impact on candidate evaluation.

References

Abramowitz, Alan I., Ronald B. Rapoport and Walter J. Stone. 1985. Nomination Choice in 1984: Caucus Attenders vs. State Convention Delegates. Presented at the annual meeting of the American Political Science Association, New Orleans.

————, and Walter J. Stone. 1984. *Nomination Politics: Party Activists and Presidential Choice.* New York: Praeger.

Aldrich, John H. 1980. *Before the Convention: Strategies and Choices in Presidential Nomination Campaigns.* Chicago: University of Chicago Press.

Aronson, Peter H., and Peter C. Ordeshook. Spatial Strategies for Sequential Elections. In Richard G. Niemi and Herbert F. Weisberg, eds., *Probability Models of Collective Decision-Making.* Columbus, OH: Charles E. Merrill.

Bartels, Larry M. 1985. Expectations and Preferences in Presidential Nominating Campaigns. *American Political Science Review*, 79:804–15.

――――. 1987. Candidate Choice and the Dynamics of the Presidential Nominating Process. *American Journal of Political Science*, 31:1–30.

Brady, Henry E. and Richard Johnston. 1987. What Is the Primary Message: Horse Race or Issue Journalism? In Gary R. Orren and Nelson W. Polsby, eds., *Media and Momentum*. Chatham, NJ: Chatham House.

Coleman, James S. 1972. The Positions of Political Parties in Elections. In Richard G. Niemi and Herbert F. Weisberg, eds., *Probability Models of Collective Decision*. Columbus, OH: Charles E. Merrill.

Downs, Anthony. 1957 *An Economic Theory of Democracy*. New York: Harper.

Hutter, James L., and Steven E. Schier. 1984. Representativeness: From Caucus to Convention in Iowa. *American Politics Quarterly*, 12:431–448.

Jackson, John S., III, Barbara Leavitt Brown and David Bositis. 1982. Herbert McClosky and Friends Revisited: 1980 Democratic and Republican Party Elites Compared to the Mass Public. *American Politics Quarterly*, 10:158–180.

Joslyn, Richard. 1984. *Mass Media and Elections*. Reading, MA: Addison-Wesley.

Keeter, Scott, and Cliff Zukin. 1983. *Uninformed Choice: The Failure of the New Presidential Nominating System*. New York: Praeger.

Kirkpatrick, Jeane. 1975. Representation in the American National Conventions: The Case of 1972. *British Journal of Political Science*, 5:265–322.

――――. 1976. *The New Presidential Elite*. New York: Russell Sage.

Lengle, James I. 1981. *Representation and Presidential Primaries: The Democratic Party in the Post-Reform Era*. Westport, CT: Greenwood.

Markus, Gregory B. 1982. Political Attitudes during an Election Year: A Report on the 1980 NES Panel Study. *American Political Science Review* 76:538–560.

――――, and Philip E. Converse. 1979. A Dynamic Simultaneous Equation Model of Electoral Choice. *American Political Science Review*, 73:1055–1070.

McClosky, Herbert, Paul J. Hoffman and Rosemary O'Hara. 1960. Issue Conflict and Consensus Among Party Leaders and Followers. *American Political Science Review*, 54:406–427.

Miller, Warren E., and M. Kent Jennings. 1986. *Parties in Transition*. New York: Russell Sage.

Montjoy, Robert S., William R. Shaffer, and Ronald E. Weber. 1980. Policy Preferences of Party Elites and Masses: Conflict or Consensus? *American Politics Quarterly*, 8:319–344.

Orren, Gary R., and Nelson W. Polsby, eds., 1987. *Media and Momentum*. Chatham, NJ: Chatham House.

Page, Benjamin I. 1978. *Choices and Echoes in Presidential Politics*. Chicago: University of Chicago Press.

Pitkin, Hannah F. 1967. *The Concept of Representation*. Berkeley: University of California Press.

Polsby, Nelson W. 1983. *Consequences of Party Reform*. New York: Oxford University Press.

Ranney, Austin. 1972. Turnout and Representation in Presidential Primary Elections. *American Political Science Review*, 66:21–37.

Rapoport, Ronald B., Alan I Abramowitz and Walter J. Stone. 1986. Groups and the Democratic Party: The 1984 Presidential Caucuses. Presented at the annual meeting of the American Political Science Association, Washington, D.C.

Roback, Thomas H. 1975. Amateurs and Professionals: Delegates to the 1972 Republican National Convention. *Journal of Politics*, 37:436–468.

Soule, John W., and James W., Clarke. 1970. Amateurs and Professionals: A Study of Delegates to the 1968 National Convention. *American Political Science Review*, 64:888–898.

Stone, Walter J. 1982. Party, Ideology, and the Lure of Victory: Iowa Activists in the 1980 Prenomination Campaign. *Western Political Quarterly*, 35 527–38.

———, and Alan I. Abramowitz. 1983. Winning May Not Be Everything, But It's More than We Thought. *American Political Science Review*, 77:945–956.

Verba, Sidney, and Norman Nie. 1972. *Participation in America*. New York: Harper.

Wildavsky, Aaron. 1965. The Goldwater Phenomenon: Purists, Politicians, and the Two-Party System. *Review of Politics*, 17:386–413.

Winebrenner, Hugh. 1987. *The Iowa Precinct Caucuses: The Making of a Media Event*. Ames: Iowa State University Press.

3

Voter Turnout
in Primary Elections

Michael G. Hagen

A central argument in opposition to the old-style method of nominating presidential candidates was that it allowed too few people to participate in making the decisions. Presidential primaries and open caucuses were the remedies of choice. And many more people now participate in the nomination process.

Nowhere near everyone participates, however. This would not be a source of concern, to scholars at least, if those who did participate were a random sample of those who could. They are not. Stone, Abramowitz and Rapoport (chapter 2) have demonstrated that presidential caucus-goers in 1984—in Iowa and elsewhere—were not entirely representative of their states' populations. Nor are primary voters very representative of their states' populations. The consequence is that the preferences of every American are not weighted equally in choosing presidential candidates.

The purpose of a chapter on primaries in a book about the Iowa caucuses is to facilitate comparison; Iowa may play a big part in the nomination process, but just a part all the same. Indeed, the fundamental argument of this chapter is that standards for comparison are prerequisite to evaluating the elements of the nomination process. If the standard against which presidential primaries are judged is a general presidential election or the pool of people registered to vote, primaries do not appear especially unrepresentative.

Research on Primary Turnout

The axioms that inform research on turnout in primary elections are the same as those that underlie research on turnout in general elections.

In primary elections as in general elections, people vote when the benefits of voting outweigh the costs. Most of the benefits of voting are expressive, not instrumental. It is probably the rare individual who is motivated to vote by a belief that his or her vote will decide an election. Instead, people vote because voting makes them feel that they have done their duty—to society, to their segment of society, to themselves—or that they have affirmed their allegiance to the political system. On the other side of the ledger, the costs of voting include the effort necessary to learn about the candidates and parties, to decide how to vote, to register, and to go to the polls on election day (Wolfinger and Rosenstone, 1980, pp. 7–8).

Neither the costs nor the benefits of voting, however, are the same in primary elections as in general elections. The costs of voting in a presidential primary are no doubt greater than the costs of voting in the general election (Aldrich, 1980, p. 81). Information about the candidates is harder to come by, especially early in the nomination campaign. There are typically more candidates about whom to become informed. Since a primary is an intraparty contest, partisanship cannot be used as a shortcut to choosing among candidates as it can in a general election. The rules governing a primary election can be complicated; the impact of a single vote on the outcome of the election can be difficult to figure. Moreover, a state's presidential primary is only one among many; the impact of a single vote on the ultimate outcome of the nomination process is even more difficult to figure and a person's vote may be rendered moot by subsequent events. Primaries are conducted by political parties on a state-by-state basis rather than by the federal government nationwide. Primaries therefore may be less likely to inspire a sense of civic duty, so the benefits of voting in a primary may be smaller than the benefits of voting in the fall. In short, primary voting is a more demanding and less rewarding task than voting in a general election.

Turnout in presidential primaries is consequently lower than turnout in general elections. Austin Ranney (1972) estimates that turnout in the 72 presidential-preference primaries held between 1948 and 1968 averaged 27 percent of the relevant state's voting-age population, compared to 62 percent in the ensuing general elections. Primary turnout has been no higher in recent years. Turnout of the voting-age population in states in which both parties held primaries was 28 percent in 1976, 25 percent in 1980 and 22 percent in 1984 (Ranney, 1977; 1981, appendix C; 1985, appendix D). Only one presidential primary since World War I has seen more than half of a state's voting-age population turn out: 55 percent voted in Oregon in 1968 (Davis, 1980). At the other extreme, turnout in Rhode Island's 1980 and 1984 primaries was little more than 6 percent (Ranney, 1981, appendix C; 1985, appendix D).

The mere fact that many Americans do not vote in presidential primaries is a source of concern to those who regard nonvoting as a sign of dissatisfaction with the political system. There exists little evidence for this interpretation in the context of general elections, however (Brody, 1978; Citrin, 1978); I know of none in the context of presidential primaries. Of much more concern to students of turnout in primaries is the question of who votes and who does not. The fundamental argument adduced in favor of primaries as a method of nominating presidential candidates holds that primaries produce candidates who are more representative of popular preferences than the candidates produced by the old methods. That argument rests on the assumption that the people who make the decisions in primaries—the voters—are more representative, in one way or another, than were the politicians who made decisions in smoke-filled rooms. The question of how representative primary voters are, therefore, has been central to most research on turnout in presidential primary elections.

Research on turnout in primary elections and the representativeness of primary electorates began with V.O. Key (1949; 1956). Key's focus was on gubernatorial, not presidential primaries, but his conclusions are worth repeating, for they have guided the subsequent generation of work on presidential primaries. Key found that primary turnout varied substantially from county to county within the states he studied. That variation was related to differences in the demographic characteristics of county populations; turnout was lower in poorer counties, for example, than in wealthier counties. From this he inferred that poorer people voted at a lower rate than wealthier people. The poor, then, and other demographic groups whose rates of voting were low, were under-represented in the voting electorate. In general, he argued, the voting electorate is a caricature, not a miniature, of the potential electorate (1949, p. 526; 1956, p. 145). If this situation persists from election to election, in Key's (1956, p. 153) oft-quoted words,

> the effective primary constituency of the state as a whole may come to consist predominantly of the people of certain sections of a state, of persons chiefly of specified national origin or religious affiliation, of people especially responsive to certain styles of political leadership or shades of ideology, or of other groups markedly unrepresentative in one way or another of the party following.

Key was the first to show that the propensity to vote in a primary is related to the demographic characteristics of individuals and that some demographic groups therefore are less well represented than others in primary electorates. Subsequent research has approached the question of "descriptive representation" from both of those angles (Pitkin, 1967, chapter 4). Looking at data on individuals, James Lengle (1980; 1981) found that turnout in the California Democratic primaries of 1968 and 1972 was higher among the better educated, the wealthier, and those in white-collar occupations, and higher among non-Hispanic whites than among racial minorities or Hispanics. Crotty and Jackson (1985) report strong relationships between 1980 primary turnout and education, income, class identification, occupational prestige, and race. In the aggregate, interstate differences in the turnout of people registered to vote in the 1976 primaries were strongly correlated with the percentage of a state's population that had some college education (Ranney, 1977). Norrander and Smith (1985) also found education to be positively related to turnout across states in 1976 and in 1980. Rothenberg and Brody (1988) found that turnout in primaries from 1952 to 1980 increased with a state's median years of education and decreased with the percentage of a state's population that was black. It is clear that some kinds of people are more likely than others to vote in presidential primaries.

So some kinds of people are clearly better represented than others in presidential primary electorates. In the 1968 primaries, voters in Wisconsin were older, had higher incomes, and worked in occupations of higher status than self-identified members of the same party who did not vote; similar differences appeared between New Hampshire voters and members of the same party who were registered but did not vote (Ranney, 1972). Democrats who voted in the 1968 and 1972 primaries in California underrepresented the poor, the poorly educated, people in blue-collar occupations, racial minorities, and Hispanics (Lengle, 1980; 1981). Nelson W. Polsby (1983, p. 159) reports that Democratic primary voters nationwide in 1976 were disproportionately high in socioeconomic class. The evidence is strong that presidential primary voters overrepresent people in the higher reaches of the society and economy and under-represent people in the lower reaches.

Demographic unrepresentativeness has political ramifications, because a number of differences in political attitudes and preferences are related to number of differences in political attitudes and preferences are related to demographic differences. Lengle (1980; 1981) examined some of these relationships among California Democrats in 1968 and 1972. The well-educated, he found, were concerned about different issues than were the poorly educated, and were also much more likely to call themselves liberals. Of even more obvious importance is the fact that preferences among the Democratic candidates were related to demographic char-acteristics among Democrats: better-educated people, wealthier people, and people in higher-status jobs were much more likely to favor Eugene McCarthy over Robert Kennedy in 1968 and George McGovern over Hubert Humphrey in 1972. Lengle (1981) went on to show that most of these relationships were also apparent in several states other than California in 1972.

If primary voters are demographically unrepresentative of the population as a whole and political preferences are related to demographic characteristics, then primary voters will be politically unrepresentative of the population. Thus New Hampshire primary voters in 1968— especially Democrats, but Republicans, too—were considerably more likely to be hawks on the Vietnam War than were their nonvoting fellow partisans; on many other issues, in New Hampshire and in Wisconsin, and in both parties, voters tended to take somewhat more extreme positions than did nonvoters (Ranney, 1972). Looking at the same relationships from another angle, Crotty and Jackson (1985) found that turnout in the 1980 primaries increased with extremity of ideological identification. People who called themselves "extremely conservative" were more likely to vote than were those who called themselves "conservative," who were in turn heavier voters than the "slightly conservative"; the pattern was the same on the liberal side. Another set of factors systematically related to primary turnout in 1980 falls under the heading of "party support." Strong party supporters and people who felt close to a party were substantially more likely to vote than were people who were not strong party supporters or did not feel close to a party. Primary voters may be unrepresentative of the issue preferences of their party's rank and file, and they certainly are on average considerably more partisan and more extreme in their ideological orientations than people who do not vote in primaries.

The political import of these differences is obvious. Lengle (1981, p. 62) concludes, for example:

> had the 1972 California Democratic primary electorate been demographically representative of the party rank and file, Hubert Humphrey, not George McGovern, almost surely would have won the primary and captured all of California's delegates to the Democratic National Convention.

Primary voters, to summarize the lessons of research on representativeness, are different from the population at large—demographically and politically. The poor, the poorly educated, the young, racial minorities, and people in lower-status occupations are underrepresented in primary electorates in comparison with their numbers in the population. Primary voters, at least in some elections, are concerned about different issues and take different positions on issues, on average, than the population as a whole. They also identify more strongly with a party and are more extreme in their ideological outlook and in their issue preferences. Most important, the distribution of candidate preferences among primary voters is, at least in some cases, not the same as the distribution of candidate preferences in the entire population. The outcomes of presidential primaries do not take into account in equal measure, therefore, the wishes of all.

Turnout and Representativeness

The fact that primary electorates are unrepresentative is often blamed on the fact that primary turnout is nearly always lower than general-election turnout. Key argued that the overall level of turnout and the composition of the voting electorate are "almost invariably" related (1949, p. 526). The percentage of people who vote, of course, varies from election to election, with the competitiveness of the race, the depth of feeling about important issues, and the actions of politicians and their organizations. The degree to which light-voting groups are under-represented, according to Key, depends on the overall level of turnout. When overall turnout is high, the extent to which low-turnout groups are underrepresented will be small; but when overall turnout is low, low-turnout groups will be severely underrepresented.

One who accepts Key's assertion and is concerned about represen-tativeness certainly must be concerned about the representativeness of primary electorates, for turnout in primaries is lower than turnout in general elections. However, the relationship between representativeness and the overall level of turnout merits careful consideration, for that relationship is more complex than it first might appear.

Given certain circumstances, turnout and representativeness are related by virtue of simple arithmetic. As a hypothetical example, consider a population of potential voters, all of whom are members of either Group A or Group B. Assume that each group makes up half of the population. Assume further that 70 percent of Group A but only 50 percent of Group B votes in the general election; because the population is evenly divided between people in the two groups, the overall rate of turnout is therefore 60 percent. In the primary election, 50 percent of Group A and 30 percent of Group B votes; the overall rate of turnout in the primary is therefore 40 percent. The difference in the turnout rates of the two groups is 20 percentage points in each election. Because the overall rate of turnout is lower in the primary than in the general election, however, Group B is underrepresented more severely in the primary electorate than in the general election electorate. Half of the people in the population are in Group B, but only 42 percent of the general election voters are and only 38 percent of the primary voters are.

The point that I would like to emphasize is how small the difference in Group B's share of the electorate is compared to the difference in overall turnout. Overall turnout is 20 percentage points lower in the primary than in the general election, yet people from Group B make up only 4 percentage points less of the primary electorate than of the general electorate. Lower overall turnout indeed leads to more severe underrepresentation of a low-turnout group—but not necessarily much more severe.

In more general terms, the impact on representativeness of a change in overall turnout depends upon the relative sizes of the groups and their rates of turnout. Figure 3.1 shows the relationship between overall turnout and a hypothetical low-turnout group's share of the voting electorate for groups of various sizes, assuming that the population consists of only two groups and that the low-turnout group votes at a rate that is twenty percentage points less than the other. The conclusion to be drawn is a simple one: a low-turnout group's share of the voting electorate will be smaller when overall turnout is less, but not much smaller unless overall turnout is very much less. The level of turnout at which a group's share of the electorate will drop precipitously depends upon the group's percentage of the population: a smaller group is less affected than a larger group by the overall level of turnout. Not shown in the figure is the fact that the level of turnout at which a group's share of the electorate will plummet also depends upon the difference between the low-turnout group's rate of turnout and the high-turnout group's rate of turnout: if the difference is larger, the low-turnout group's share of the electorate will fall more quickly at a higher level of overall turnout. Even when that difference is 20 percentage points, however, the extent to which the low-turnout group is underrepresented in the voting electorate does not change much until turnout is substantially below 30 percent.

The purpose of this exercise is to illustrate the complexities of the relationship about which Key wrote. Voters in a primary may be nearly as representative of the population as are voters in a general election in which twice as many people vote; it depends on the absolute rates of turnout in the two elections. Accurate estimates of the rates of turnout in primaries and in general elections are therefore essential to judging the potential for primary voters to be less representative than general-election voters.

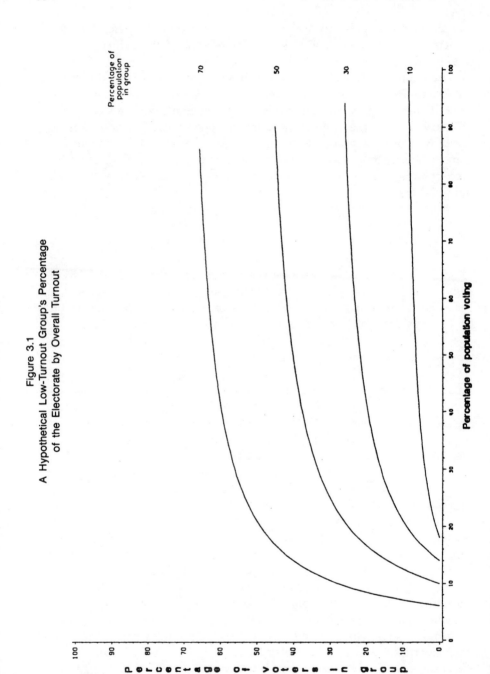

Figure 3.1
A Hypothetical Low-Turnout Group's Percentage
of the Electorate by Overall Turnout

Primary Turnout in 1976

The best available data on voter turnout in recent years are from the Current Population Survey (CPS) conducted by the U.S. Bureau of the Census. The CPS is a monthly survey of the nation's civilian noninstitutional population. In the survey following each general election since 1964, the CPS has included questions about whether people were registered and voted in the November election. In 1976, for the first and only time, the survey included a question about voting in a primary election.

The CPS includes no information about any other political attitudes or activities, but it offers several advantages over conventional sample surveys for studying turnout. Foremost among these is the size of the sample. The 1976 CPS conducted personal interviews in 45,000 households. In each household, where possible, every person age 14 or older was interviewed; information about household members who could not be interviewed was provided by proxy.[1] The result, excluding those too young to vote, is a national sample consisting of approximately 89,000 individuals. This enormous sample provides an opportunity for extraordinarily precise estimates of turnout—for the population as a whole and for subgroups of the population.[2]

Estimates of 1976 primary turnout in seven states based upon the CPS are presented on Table 3.1.[3] For comparison, Table 3.1 includes Ranney's (1977) estimates as well. Those figures put turnout across the seven states at 28.1 percent, ranging from 11.7 percent in New Jersey to 37.3 percent in California (Table 3.1, column 1). The CPS figures are much higher. Judging from the CPS, 43.7 percent of the voting-age population of the seven states in the sample voted in a presidential primary election in 1976. The state rates of turnout range from 33.4 percent in New Jersey to over 48 percent in Pennsylvania, Indiana, and California (Table 3.1, column 2).

Discrepancies between estimates of turnout among the voting-age population based on the CPS and estimates like those Ranney presents have been explained in detail elsewhere (Wolfinger and Rosenstone, 1980, appendix A; Hagen, 1988). In brief, Ranney's figures are calculated as the Census Bureau calculates the "official" turnout figures for general elections—dividing the total number of votes counted, as reported by election officials, by the total resident voting-age population. For several reasons, the numerator in this calculation understates the number of people who actually voted and the denominator severely overstates, as Ranney notes (1977, pp. 17–18), the size of the voting-age population. Primary turnout in 1976 therefore was undoubtedly higher than Ranney's figures indicate.

TABLE 3.1   Estimates of Voter Turnout in Seven 1976 Primary Elections (Percent Voting)

	Votes Cast by Voting-Age Population[a]	Self-Reported Turnout of Voting-Age Population[b]	Self-Reported Turnout of Voting Age Citizens[c]	Votes Cast by Registered[d]	Self-Reported Turnout Registered[e]
California	37.3	48.0	53.1	74.1	73.5
Illinois	27.0	41.7	43.7	36.3	53.4
Indiana	34.2	48.1	49.2	42.8	62.4
New Jersey	11.7	33.4	35.5	17.2	45.6
Ohio	27.9	43.5	44.4	na	62.6
Pennsylvania	25.9	48.2	49.4	43.5	70.5
Texas	23.3	37.9	40.0	36.9	56.8
Total	28.1	43.7	46.2	52.5	62.6

[a]Calculated by dividing the total number of votes counted by the Census Bureau's estimate of the total voting-age population. Reported in Ranney (1977). Total recalculated for the seven states.
[b]Estimated from the 1976 Current Population Survey. Excludes respondents whose primary voting was not ascertained and those who did not know whether they had voted in a primary.
[c]Estimated from the 1976 Current Population Survey. Excludes in addition respondents whose citizenship was not ascertained.
[d]Calculated by dividing the total number of votes counted by the number of people on state voter registration rolls. Reported in Ranney (1977). Number of registered voters in Ohio not available. Total recalculated for the seven states.
[e]Estimated from the 1976 Current Population Survey. Excludes in addition respondents who did not know whether they were registered or whose registration was not ascertained.

Estimates of turnout calculated on the basis of the CPS escape most of these problems. The CPS estimates of primary turnout do overstate to some extent the number of people who actually voted and understate slightly the size of the voting-age population; it would be prudent to conclude that primary turnout in 1976 was probably a bit lower than the CPS figures indicate. Largely because the CPS figures are based on a better estimate of the size of the voting-age population, however, primary turnout in 1976 was undoubtedly closer to the CPS figures than to Ranney's.[4]

Moreover, the CPS data have the advantage of allowing a large group of people who are not eligible to vote to be removed from the sample. Turnout rates based upon the voting-age population underestimate turnout among the people legally eligible to participate: U.S. citizens (Wolfinger and Rosenstone, 1980, pp. 115–116). Noncitizens made up a substantial share of the voting-age populations of the seven states analyzed here. The percentage of noncitizens ranged from 0.8 in Indiana to 8.6 in California—4.1 percent overall. Because noncitizens cannot vote, removing them increases the estimated rates of turnout. Just over 53 percent of the citizens in California voted in the 1976 primary, a figure 5.1 percentage points higher than the CPS estimate for the voting-age population. The lowest figure is again for New Jersey, where 35.5 percent of the citizens voted in the primary (Table 3.1, column 3). Over the seven states, the turnout rate of citizens was 46.2 percent. Primary turnout was indeed lower than turnout in the general election; 65 percent of the citizens in the seven states, according to the CPS, voted in November of 1976. Even allowing for some upward bias in the estimates, however, it is certainly not the case that only a tiny fraction of citizens in these seven states participated in 1976 presidential primaries.

Citizenship is not the only legal impediment to voting; registration is another. Ranney's data indicate that in five of the six states for which he had data, less than half of those already registered voted in a primary (Table 3.1, column 4). Only in California did a majority of the registered turn out. The CPS estimates again are substantially higher—for the same reasons as before, plus an additional one. State registration rolls, the basis for Ranney's estimates, are not a very accurate source of data about the number of people actually registered to vote in a particular election; they contain a substantial amount of "deadwood"—people who have moved or died (Squire, Wolfinger, and Glass, 1987, pp. 46–47). The upshot is that Ranney's figures, because they are based on an inflated estimate of the number registered to vote, understate turnout among the registered. The CPS data also probably overstate the number of people registered for the primaries somewhat.[5] Nonetheless, the CPS estimates of the primary turnout of those registered to vote are much higher than Ranney's. Across the seven states, 62.6 percent of the registered voted in a primary (Table 3.1, column 5). In only one state— New Jersey, where 45.6 percent voted—did a majority of the registered fail to vote. In both California and Pennsylvania, more than 70 percent of the registered turned out. Given the large gap between the percentage of citizens voting and the percentage of the registered voting—16.4 percentage points, judging from the CPS—registration is apparently a formidable barrier to voting in primaries, as it is to voting in general elections (Campbell, et al., 1960, pp. 277–280; Kelley, Ayres, and Bowen, 1967; Kim, Petrocik, and Enokson, 1975; Wolfinger and Rosenstone, 1980, chapter 4; Squire, Wolfinger, and Glass, 1987). To be sure, a smaller percentage of the registered in these seven states voted in the primaries than in the general election; 91 percent of the registered voted in November. But even in the primary elections, in these states at least, most of those who were registered voted.

The CPS estimates, then, paint a much different picture than do Ranney's estimates of the overall levels of turnout in the 1976 primaries

for which both estimates are available. Using better data on the size of
the voting-age population and excluding noncitizens puts the overall
rate of turnout at 46.2 percent, rather than 28.1 percent. Even allowing
for the possibility that the CPS figure exaggerates turnout slightly, that
rate of turnout should be of some comfort to those who watched turnout
figures in the aftermath of Watergate for signs that the American political
system was disintegrating. More to the point, the fact that the fraction
of citizens who voted in these seven primaries is closer to one-half than
to one-quarter leads to very different expectations about the extent to
which low-turnout groups were underrepresented in these 1976 primary
electorates. Unless group differences in turnout are very large, accepting
the assumptions of the hypothetical example discussed above, underrepresentation in an election in which 46 percent of the citizens take
part is not necessarily much more severe than in an election in which
65 percent of the citizens take part—as in the general election of 1976.
In fact, underrepresentation in a voting electorate that includes 46 percent
of the citizens may not be much more severe than in a potential electorate
that includes 72 percent of the citizens—those who were registered to
vote in 1976.

Demographic Characteristics,
Registration, and Turnout in 1976

Judging from the CPS estimates for 1976 and the hypothetical example
discussed above, it does not seem that turnout in primary elections is
so much lower than turnout in general elections that primary voters are
inevitably much less representative than general-election voters. Nonetheless, it may be the case empirically that primary voters are much
less representative than general-election voters, for the hypothetical
example assumed that group differences in turnout were the same in
low-turnout elections as in high-turnout elections. That assumption may
not fit the facts. If group differences in turnout are greater in primaries
than in general elections, primary voters will be much less representative
than general-election voters.

Table 3.2 displays the 1976 registration and turnout rates of a number
of demographic groups in the CPS seven-state sample. It is plain that
differences between the turnout rates in primaries and in the general
election are, for the most part, no greater among those relatively unlikely
to vote than among those relatively likely to vote. In fact, the difference
between general-election turnout and primary turnout is greater among
the well educated than among the poorly educated, greater among the
wealthier than among the poorer, greater among nonblacks than among
blacks, and greater among non-Hispanics than among Hispanics (Table

TABLE 3.2   Registration, General-Election Turnout and Primary Turnout in Seven States by Demographic Characteristics, 1976 Current Population Survey (in Percent)[a]

	Registered	General Election	Primary	Primary Minus Registered	Primary Minus General Election
Years of School Completed					
0 - 11	61	54	37	-24	-17
12	72	65	44	-28	-21
13+	85	80	57	-28	-23
Family Income					
$0-$10,000	64	56	38	-26	-18
$10,000-$14,999	71	64	44	-27	-20
$15,000-$24,999	80	75	53	-27	-22
$25,000+	88	83	59	-29	-24
Age					
18-34	62	55	31	-31	-24
35-49	79	74	54	-25	-20
50-64	84	78	60	-24	-18
65+	79	71	55	-24	-16
Women	73	66	45	-28	-21
Men	73	67	47	-26	-20
Blacks	71	62	44	-27	-18
Non-Blacks	73	67	46	-27	-21
Hispanics	55	47	32	-23	-15
Non-Hispanics	74	68	47	-27	-21

[a]Includes only U.S. citizens age 18 and over for whom complete demographic and voting information is available.

3.2, column 5). The only low-turnout group whose voting rate falls more from the general election to the primary than its counterpart is young people. What is more, differences between the registration rates and turnout rates in primaries are also, for the most part, no greater among those relatively unlikely to vote than among those relatively likely to vote. Young people are again the exception, as are, to a small degree, women. In 1976, at least, it certainly was not the case that groups with relatively low rates of registration and relatively low rates of turnout in the general election had relatively low rates of turnout by an even wider margin in primaries.

This result may be examined from another angle. Comparing the rows of Table 3.2 reveals the bivariate relationship between each of these demographic variables and registration and turnout. These relationships are all in the directions that previous research on turnout would suggest. The point to notice is that the relationships are weaker with respect to primary turnout than with respect to general-election turnout. The best educated, for example, were 26 percentage points more likely than the least educated to vote in the general election, but only 20 percentage points more likely to vote in a primary. The wealthiest were 27 percentage points more likely than the poorest to vote in the general election, 21 percentage points more likely to vote in a primary. Again, age was the only exceptional factor. All of the other demographic characteristics were substantially more strongly related to turnout in the general election than to turnout in the primaries.

This result is not the product of the relationships among the demographic variables; it is confirmed by multivariate analysis. I employed a rather simple model to assess the independent effects of a number of factors on registration, general-election turnout, and primary turnout in 1976. Included among the explanatory variables are seven demographic characteristics and the state's closing date for registration.[6] The demographic variables are education, age, income, gender, race, Hispanicity, and the length of time a respondent had lived at his or her current address.[7] These are certainly not all the demographic characteristics that could have been included, but they are the ones that most previous research agrees have the biggest impact on turnout. Table 3.3 reports the results for education, income, and age.[8]

Other things being equal, education had an enormous impact on the likelihood that an individual would vote in the 1976 primaries. A person who had completed eight years of elementary school was 13 percentage points more likely to vote than a person with fewer than five years of school (Table 3.3). People who had high school diplomas were another 11 percentage points more likely to vote and people with college degrees were yet another 16 percentage points more likely. These are very large differences. But the difference between the most educated and the least educated is smaller with respect to primary turnout than with respect to registration and turnout in the general election. College graduates, for example, were 48 percentage points more likely to be registered and 48 percentage points more likely to vote in the general election than were the least educated, but only 40 percentage points more likely to vote in a primary.[9]

The differences among income categories in primary turnout are no larger than the differences in registration and general-election turnout. People with family incomes between $10,000 and $15,000 were only 4

TABLE 3.3 Effects of Education, Family Income and Age on Registration, General-Election Turnout and Primary-Election Turnout in Seven States, Controlling for Other Demographic Characteristics and Registration Closing Date, 1976 Current Population Survey[a]

	Registered	General Election	Primary
Years of School Completed[b]			
5-7	6	5	6
8	13	13	13
9-11	21	20	18
12	31	29	24
13-15	42	40	30
16	48	48	40
17+	52	54	49
Family Income[c]			
$5,000-$9,999	3	3	2
$10,000-$14,999	6	7	4
$15,000-$19,999	8	9	6
$20,000-$24,999	9	11	8
$25,000-$49,999	10	13	10
$50,000+	9	11	11
Age[d]			
20-24	6	6	5
25-29	12	13	11
30-34	17	19	18
35-39	21	23	24
40-44	23	26	29
45-49	26	29	33
50-54	28	31	36
55-59	30	33	38
60-64	33	35	38
65-69	36	36	37
70+	37	35	34

[a]Includes only U.S. citizens age 18 and over for whom complete demographic and voting information is available. The number in each cell is the logit estimate of the difference in percentage registered or percentage turnout (calculated from the parameter estimates in Appendix C) associated with being in the category specified rather than being in the base category.
[b]Base category: Fewer that five years of school.
[c]Base category: Family income less that $5,000.
[d]Base category: Age 18-19 years old.

percentage points more likely to vote in a 1976 primary than were people with family incomes less than $5000, compared to differences of 6 percentage points with respect to registration and 7 points with respect to turnout in November (Table 3.3). Primary and general-election turnout rise equally with increases in income from $15,000 to just under $50,000, going up a total of 6 percentage points; the registration rate rises slightly less, 4 percentage points. Overall, the result is clear: differences between the financially well-off and the poor are no larger for primary turnout than for registration and general-election turnout.

The differences I found in the registration, general-election turnout, and primary turnout rates of three other pairs of demographic groups are similarly unimpressive, other things being equal. Blacks, with these other factors held constant, were 6 percentage points more likely to vote in a primary than were whites and people of other races; blacks were only 4 percentage points more likely to vote in the general election, 6 percentage points more likely to be registered.[10] Hispanics were 1 percentage point more likely to vote in the primaries than were people of other ethnic origins, while they were 1 percentage point less likely to be registered and 3 percentage points less likely to vote in the general election.[11] And women were only 1 percentage point less likely than men to vote in a primary and only 1 percentage point more likely to be registered and to vote in the fall.

In a multivariate context as in the bivariate context, age is demographic characteristic that appears to be more strongly related to primary turnout than to registration or turnout in the general election. From age 18 to age 29, primary turnout rises slightly more slowly than do registration and general election turnout. The difference in the turnout rates of teenagers and of people in their late twenties is 11 percentage points in the primaries, 12 percentage points in registration, and 13 points in the general election (Table 3.3). From age 30 to age 60, turnout in the primaries rises more rapidly than does turnout in November, and much more rapidly than does registration. The biggest disparity is among people in their early fifties. The difference between that group and the youngest group is 5 percentage points larger in primary turnout than in general-election turnout and 8 percentage points larger in primary turnout than in registration. The likelihood of voting turns down some- what past one's seventieth birthday, a little more in the 1976 primaries than in the 1976 general election. The elderly aside, age differences in primary turnout appear to be larger than age differences in registration or general-election turnout.[12]

In sum, group differences in primary turnout in 1976 were for the most part no greater than group differences in registration and turnout in the general election. To put the same conclusion another way:

differences between turnout in the primaries, on the one hand, and registration and turnout in the general election, on the other, were for the most part no greater among low-turnout groups than among high-turnout groups.

It is true that some of the group differences in primary turnout in 1976 were very large, larger than the 20 percentage-point difference assumed in the hypothetical example displayed in Figure 3.1. As I noted in discussing that example, the degree to which low-turnout groups are underrepresented in lower-turnout elections will increase with larger group differences in turnout, other things being equal. It is worth considering the turnout rates of the various demographic groups again to see why at least one other thing, in this case, is not equal.

The thing is that differences between primary turnout and general-election turnout in 1976 were in many cases substantially smaller among low-turnout groups than among high-turnout groups. Among people with fewer than 12 years of education, for example, primary turnout was only 17 percentage points lower than general-election turnout, compared to a difference of 23 percentage points among those with more than 12 years of school (Table 3.2). People with family incomes under $10,000 were only 18 percentage points less likely to vote in the primary than in the fall, compared to a difference of 24 points among those with family incomes of $25,000 or more. One interpretation of this result is that there is a hard core of people, even in the low-turnout groups, who will vote in any election.[13] As a consequence, there is a threshold below which the turnout rates of the low-turnout groups cannot fall; unless the number of hard-core people in the high-turnout group is much larger than the number in the low-turnout group, the turnout rate of the high-turnout group can fall farther.[14] Whether this interpretation is correct or not, the fact is that the smaller differences among low-turnout than among high-turnout groups in primary versus general-election turnout in 1976 counterbalance to some extent the magnitude of the group differences in primary turnout. In short, it still may be that voters in the primaries were as representative as voters in the general election.

The Representativeness of
Primary Voters in 1976

From the fact that turnout in the 1976 primary elections was heavily influenced by the demographic characteristics of citizens it follows that some groups of citizens defined by their demographic characteristics were underrepresented in the primary electorate. But registration and turnout in the general election of 1976, as presumably in all elections,

TABLE 3.4   Demographic Characteristics of Citizens, Citizens Registered to Vote, General-Election Voters and Primary Voters in Seven States, 1976 Current Population Survey (in Percent)[a]

	Voting-Age Citizens	Registered	General Election	Primary	Primary Minus Voting-Age Citizens	Primary Minus Registered	Primary Minus General Election
Years of School Completed							
0-11	29	25	24	23	-6	-1	0
12	39	39	38	38	-1	-1	0
13+	32	37	38	39	+7	+2	+1
Family Income							
$0-$9,999	36	32	30	30	-6	-1	-1
$10,000-$14,999	25	24	24	24	-1	-1	0
$15,000-$24,999	27	30	31	31	+4	+1	+1
$25,000+	12	15	15	16	+3	+1	0
Age							
18-34	40	34	33	27	-13	-7	-6
35-49	24	26	26	28	+4	+2	+2
50-64	22	25	26	29	+7	+3	+3
65+	14	15	15	16	+3	+2	+2
Women	54	54	53	53	-1	-1	-1
Blacks	9	8	8	8	0	0	0
Hispanics	5	4	4	4	-2	0	0

[a]Includes only U.S. citizens age 18 and over for whom complete demographic and voting information is available. Due to rounding error, some of the distributions do not total exactly 100, some of the differences reported do not equal exactly the differences between distributions, and some of the differences do not total exactly 0.

were also heavily influenced by demographic characteristics. Therefore, although it is noted much less frequently, people who are registered and people who vote in general elections also are not perfectly representative of all citizens.[15]

Table 3.4 compares the demographic representativeness, in the seven-state CPS sample, of those registered to vote, those who voted in the 1976 general election, and those who voted in a 1976 primary. The last three columns of the table show the differences between each demographic group's share of the primary electorate and its share of citizens, the registered, and general-election voters, respectively. Primary voters were not representative of all citizens: the poorly educated, the young, and those with lower incomes were underrepresented. The difference between the percentage of primary voters with no more than a high-school education and the percentage of citizens with no more than a high-school education is a total of 7 points. The difference between the percentage of primary voters with family incomes under $15,000 and the percentage of citizens with family incomes under $15,000 is also 7 points. And the difference between the percentage of primary voters under the age of 35 and the percentage of citizens under the age of 35 is 13 points. Hispanics were somewhat underrepresented, women slightly underrepresented, and blacks not at all.[16]

Given the past research on primary voters, these results cannot be surprising; there is widespread agreement in the literature that primary electorates are unrepresentative of the population. What is noteworthy is that primary voters in these seven states were hardly at all less representative of citizens than were general-election voters. In fact, primary voters were in most respects quite representative of all the people who were registered to vote. The difference between the percentage of primary voters with no more than a high-school education and the percentage of the registered with no more than a high-school education is a total of 2 points; primary voters were hardly different at all from general-election voters in their level of education. The difference between the percentage of primary voters with family incomes under $15,000 and the percentage of the registered voters with family incomes under $15,000 is also 2 percentage points; the difference with respect to general-election voters is only 1 percentage point. Women, blacks, and Hispanics were only very slightly underrepresented in the primary electorate in comparison to the registered or in comparison to the November electorate. Only the young were decidedly more absent from the primary electorate than from the ranks of the registered and general-election voters. The differences between the percentage of primary voters under the age of 35 and the percentages of the registered and of general-election voters under the age of 35 are 7 and 6 points, respectively.

With the single exception of youth, primary voters in these seven states in 1976 were extraordinarily representative of voters in the general election, and quite representative of all the people who were registered to vote in 1976.

Residential Mobility, Registration, and Turnout

The slight degree to which primary voters in 1976 were unrepresentative of general-election voters and of people registered to vote may be due to two somewhat pedestrian factors. Changing addresses close to election day has been shown to reduce substantially an American's probability of voting in a general election (Wolfinger and Rosenstone, 1980, pp. 50–54; Squire, Wolfinger, and Glass, 1987). The main reason is that people who move must re-register to vote, and some do not do so. General-election turnout is also reduced where state law requires people to register further in advance of the election (Rosenstone and Wolfinger, 1978; Wolfinger and Rosenstone, 1980, p. 71). Knowing when to vote is easy; headlines herald the arrival of the appointed day, campaign workers call, flags fly; considerably less hoopla signals the deadline for registering to vote. The further the closing date is from election day, the greater the number of people who find themselves unregistered when it is too late—after the registration deadline has passed.

The two factors interact. The effects of moving depend, at least to some extent, on the registration requirements of the state to which one moves; where registration is easier, the impact of moving is somewhat smaller. And the effect of the closing date on the likelihood that a person will vote depends upon how recently the person has moved (Squire, Wolfinger, and Glass, 1987, pp. 55–57). I investigated here the effects of the length of time that a person had lived at the same address and the length of time before an election that he or she was required to register on registration, general-election turnout, and primary turnout. The effects were estimated separately and in interaction, with the effects of other demographic characteristics controlled. The results are in Table 3.5.[17]

The effects of having to register further in advance of an election on turnout in the 1976 primary elections and in the 1976 general election are manifest. The magnitude of the effect depends upon how recently people had moved. Among people who had lived at the same address for two years or less, a closing date of 13 days rather than 40 days increased primary turnout and general-election turnout by 6 to 7 percentage points. Among people at the same address for six or more years, however, the closing date had no effect on turnout in the fall; all of the people who had not moved in the previous six years but nonetheless needed to re-register—in most states the only reason would be failing to vote in an election or two—were apparently prompted to do so well in advance of the 1976 general election. The same is not true with regard to the primary elections. Even among the people at the same address for six or more years, primary turnout was 2 to 3 percentage points lower where the closing date was 13 days than where it was 40 days. The excitement of an election—or at least widespread knowledge that an election is approaching—apparently does not precede the day of a primary by as much as it does the day of a general election. This makes perfect sense in light of differences in the lengths of the two kinds of campaigns; except in Iowa, the campaign for a state's delegates to a party's convention begins much closer to the date of the election than does the fall campaign.

The evidence for registration is more puzzling. Among people who had lived at the same address for less than three years, the effect of

TABLE 3.5 Effects of Residential Mobility and Residential Closing Date on Registration, General-Election Turnout and Primary-Election Turnout in Seven States, Controlling for Other Demographic Characteristics, 1976 Current Population Survey[a]

	Registration Closing Date	Registration	General Election	Primary Election
Less Than 1 Month	40	--	--	--
	31	1	2	2
	28	2	3	3
	13	5	7	6
1-6 Months	40	0	0	0
	31	2	3	2
	28	2	4	3
	13	5	7	6
7-11 Months	40	2	2	1
	31	3	4	3
	28	4	5	4
	13	6	8	7
1-2 Years	40	2	2	1
	31	5	6	5
	28	5	6	6
	13	7	9	9
3-5 Years	40	10	10	9
	31	10	11	11
	28	10	11	11
	13	10	13	14
6-9 Years	40	18	18	18
	31	17	19	19
	28	16	17	19
	13	14	18	21
10 Years or More	40	21	22	24
	31	21	23	25
	28	19	22	25
	13	16	21	26

[a]Includes only U.S. citizens age 18 and over for whom complete demographic and voting information is available. The number in each cell is the logit estimate of the difference in percentage registered or percentage turnout (calculated from the parameter estimates in Appendix C) associated with being in the mobility category specified rather than having lived in the same residence for less than one month and in a state with a closing date of 40 days.

the closing date is substantial—3 to 5 percentage points—but smaller than the effect on turnout in the primary or general elections. Among those living at the same address for six years or more, the effect of the closing date on registration appears to be negative. I can think of no plausible substantive explanation.[18] My guess is that the failure of the CPS survey to ask whether people were registered to vote at their current address and the overreporting of registration by recent movers that probably resulted are at least partly responsible for the odd estimates of the impact of closing dates on registration.[19]

The effect of moving on primary turnout in 1976 was large, especially where the closing date was longer, and somewhat larger than the effect on general-election turnout. Among people who lived where the closing date was 13 days, people who had lived at the same address for three to five years were 8 percentage points more likely than people at the same address for a month or less to vote in a primary, compared to a difference of 6 percentage points with respect to voting in the general election.[20] Where the closing date was forty days, the parallel figures are 9 percent for primary turnout and 10 percent for general-election turnout. Primary voting among people living at the same address for ten years or more was another 12 to 15 percentage points higher, compared to a further increase in general-election voting of 8 to 12 percentage points.

Having moved recently thus appears to reduce primary turnout even more than turnout in the general election. This is consistent with Wolfinger and Rosenstone's conclusion (1980, p. 53) that the effects of moving are counteracted more quickly when a presidential election comes along than when a mid-term election does. A presidential election apparently motivates more movers to re-register than a mid-term election does. The results here refine that conclusion a little. The effects of moving are reduced more by a general election than by a primary. A presidential primary apparently motivates fewer movers to re-register than a general presidential election does.

Registration Requirements
and Representativeness

Turnout in 1976 primaries was affected by the length of time before the election that one was required to register. Primary voters in 1976 were more representative of citizens who were registered to vote than of all citizens. Thus registration requirements evidently have a lot to do with primary turnout and, therefore, with the fact that primary electorates do not represent all citizens equally. If one wanted to increase the representativeness of primary electorates in comparison to the nation's citizens, a place to start is by removing the obstacles to registration that hit hardest the groups that are underrepresented.

As Squire, Wolfinger, and Glass (1987) demonstrate, the largest of the groups whose turnout is heavily impeded by registration requirements consists of those who change their places of residence within a year or two of the election. The percentage of the population that moves in the period between any two national elections is startlingly large; between the years 1978 and 1980, 29 percent of voting-age citizens moved (Squire, Wolfinger, and Glass, 1987, p. 46). Movers are not, however, a cross-section of the population. People who moved between 1978 and 1980, for example, were substantially younger and marginally poorer than people who had not moved (Squire, Wolfinger, and Glass, 1987, p. 48). Moreover, even with the effects of demographic characteristics held constant, the effects of moving on general-election turnout fall more heavily on some segments of the population than on others (Wolfinger and Rosenstone, 1980, p. 54; Squire, Wolfinger, and Glass, 1987, pp. 53–55).

Moving impedes voting, for the most part, because movers must re-register themselves at their new addresses; absent this requirement, more people would vote. Squire and his colleagues (1987) estimated the impact on general-election turnout of a proposal to re-register automatically at their new addresses people who move within a state. If the impact of moving were removed, these scholars calculate, turnout in the general election of 1980 would have been increased by 9 percentage points. The political impact of such a change, they found, would have been virtually nil. Due to the relationship between residential mobility and demographic characteristics, however, re-registering movers automatically would have some consequences for the demographic character of the general electorate: it would be somewhat younger, slightly less well educated, and slightly poorer. The groups whose shares of the general electorate would be increased, that is, are precisely those groups of citizens who are under-represented in primary electorates. Given that residential mobility had an even larger impact on turnout in the 1976 primaries than on turnout in the 1976 general election, it makes sense to examine the effect of the proposed change in registration arrangements on primary turnout.

The impact of re-registering movers automatically on the demographic composition of the registered, the fall electorate, and the primary electorate in 1976 can be estimated by calculating what each individual's probability of registering or voting would be if he or she had lived at the same address for ten years or more. The differences I calculated between the composition of the 1976 primary electorate predicted by the multivariate model and the electorate projected by the model with the effects of residential mobility removed are shown on Table 3.6.[21]

TABLE 3.6   Differences Between Predicted Demographic Characteristics and Projected
                Demographic Characteristics of Citizens Registered to Vote, General-Election
                Voters and Primary Voters in Seven States, Assuming 10 or More Years at
                the Same Address, 1976 Current Population Survey (in Percent)ª

	Registration	General-Election	Primary-Election
Years of School Completed			
0-11	+1	0	0
12	+1	+1	0
13+	-1	-1	0
Family Income			
$0-$9,999	+1	+1	+1
$10,000-$14,999	0	0	0
$15,000-$24,999	-1	-1	-1
$25,000+	-1	-1	-1
Age			
18-34	+3	+4	+5
35-49	-1	-1	-1
50-64	-2	-2	-3
65+	-1	-1	-1
Women	0	0	0
Blacks	0	0	0
Hispanics	0	0	0

ªIncludes only U.S. citizens age 18 and over for whom complete demographic and voting
information is available. Each entry is the specified group's percentage in the projected
registered or electorate minus the group's percentage in the predicted registered or electorate.
Due to rounding error, some of the differences across education, income and age do not total
exactly 0.

If movers were not required to re-register, the group most strongly
affected would be the young—the group most severely underrepresented
in the primaries. The percentage of the primary electorate that consisted
of people age 18 to 34 would rise 5 percentage points. Another group
underrepresented in the primary electorate in 1976—people in families
with incomes under $15,000—would also gain a bit, although only
between 1 and 2 percentage points. The representativeness of the primary
electorate with respect to education, gender, race, and Hispanicity would
be unchanged. A similar pattern of changes in the representation of the
young and the poor among the registered and among general-election
voters is predicted, so the representativeness of the primary electorate
in comparison with the registered and the general electorate would be
changed by less than the representativeness of the primary electorate
in comparison with all citizens. Changes in the age distribution would
be larger, however, among primary voters than among the registered
and general-election voters, so that the primary electorate would be
more representative of those two groups with respect to the only

demographic group of registered people and general-election voters that is substantially underrepresented in the primary electorate, the young. In short, the primary electorates of 1976 would have been, to a marked extent, even more representative of the nation's citizens and slightly more representative of the registered and of general-election voters had the requirement that recent movers re-register been removed.

Conclusion

The literature on voter turnout in presidential primary elections makes much of the fact that primaries do not weigh the preferences of all citizens equally, because all citizens are not equally likely to vote in primaries. One defense of primaries as a means of choosing presidential candidates, in the face of strong evidence that primary electorates are not demographically representative of all citizens, is that demographic representation and political representation are not the same things. The question of how demographic characteristics and political preferences are related is not altogether settled, but research on the impact of self-interest on political opinions certainly suggests that particular socio-economic circumstances do not always translate into particular policy preferences (Green, 1985).

One of the controversies in the literature on primary turnout concerns whom primary voters ought to represent. Should the primary electorate be representative of the population as a whole? Should the voters in a party's primary be representative of people who identify with that party in that state? Of people who are registered as members of the party? Of card-carrying members? Less attention has been paid, I think, to the standard against which the representativeness of presidential primaries is judged. If less than 100 percent of a state's citizens vote and some kinds of people are less likely to vote than others, as V.O. Key noted, some kinds of people will be underrepresented. How representative, then, must a primary electorate be in order to be a valued part of a democratic process? Compared to what?

Generalizing from one year's primaries in seven states is risky business. Several caveats are in order. The first is that the seven states for which I was able to obtain data on primary turnout are, in an important respect, very different from the rest of the country and from the rest of the states that hold presidential primaries: they are bigger.[22] One consequence is that presidential candidates devote more of their attention and other resources to those states; Gurian (1986) has shown, for example, that candidates for a presidential nomination spend more money in states with larger convention delegations. Lavish spending may increase primary turnout, and it may increase the turnout of some demographic groups more than others (Ranney, 1977; Norrander and Smith, 1985). I cannot test this speculation with the CPS data because the candidates in 1976 spent heavily in all seven states in the primary sample (Aldrich, 1980).[23] So the conclusions that I draw may not apply to every other state.

It is also true that my conclusions may not apply to every other election year. In 1976 there were spirited contests for each party's presidential nomination, between Ford and Reagan on the Republican side, between Carter and a host of others on the Democratic side. For the same reasons that heavy spending may alter the composition of the voting electorate, a big field and a close race may alter it as well (Zeidenstein, 1970; Morris and Davis, 1975; Ranney, 1977; Moran and Fenster, 1982; Schier, 1982; Rothenberg and Brody, 1988). Then, too, the general election of 1976 was perhaps atypical, for that election saw a low point in presidential-election turnout. Turnout in 1976 probably was close enough to turnout in other recent presidential elections, however, to suggest that the results I report here may apply to other elections as well.

In any election, all citizens are not equally likely to vote. Indeed, all citizens are not equally likely to be registered to vote. The analysis reported here suggests that, in most respects, demographic differences in primary turnout are much the same as demographic differences in general-election turnout and in registration—perhaps smaller. The result is that primary electorates are very nearly representative of the general electorate and are quite representative of people registered to vote. The requirements of registration are responsible for a great deal of the demographic unrepresentativeness of primary voters in comparison with the nation's citizens. Easing the burden of registration would make primary voters even more representative of general-election voters, of those registered to vote, and, especially, of all citizens.

Appendix A: The Seven-State CPS Sample

If the CPS has an enormous virtue, the 1976 CPS has its faults as well, particularly for studying voting in presidential primaries. A few of these limit the scope of the analysis.

The 1976 CPS includes unique identifying codes for only 12 states and the District of Columbia. Of these, 11 held presidential primaries for both parties in 1976. (There was no Republican primary in the District of Columbia in 1976 and Connecticut selected convention delegates in caucuses.) The remaining states are combined into ten groups, none of which consists entirely of states that held primaries. The number of states available for analysis is limited further by the fact that the question used to assess primary turnout asked whether the respondent had voted "earlier this year in a primary election to determine the candidate for Congress or President." People who voted in a congressional primary therefore cannot be distinguished from people who voted in a presidential primary. Many states, of course, hold congressional and presidential primaries on the same day; four of the 11, however, held nonconcurrent congressional and presidential primaries in 1976. In order to be certain that people who answered the question in the affirmative were saying that they had gone to the polls on the day of the presidential primary, I have restricted the analysis here to the seven identifiable states that held concurrent congressional and presidential primaries in 1976: California, Illinois, Indiana, New Jersey, Ohio, Pennsylvania, and Texas. This restriction leaves the number of individuals whose registration and turnout can be assessed at slightly more than 35,000.

Residents of the seven states in the sample analyzed here were not precisely like residents of the other 43 in their demographic characteristics, but they were not very different either. The biggest difference, as one might expect when comparing some of the largest states to the rest, is that a much larger share of the seven-state sample lived in a large metropolitan area, 79 percent to 60 percent. The seven-state sample is a bit better educated and a bit better off financially: 30 percent of the people in the seven-state sample did not finish high school, compared to 32 percent elsewhere; 36 percent, compared to 43 percent, had family incomes under $10,000. Because California and Texas are among the states included, a larger percentage of the seven-state sample is Hispanic (5 percent) than in the remainder (2 percent). Because the South is by and large excluded, the percentage of blacks in the seven-state sample (9 percent) is slightly smaller than the percentage elsewhere (11 percent). With respect to the political activities that can be assessed in both samples, however, the two are very much alike. Seventy-two percent of the respondents in the seven states said that they were registered to vote, compared to 74 percent of the others. Sixty-five percent in the sample voted in the general election, compared to 66 percent of the others. (All of these figures are based on respondents who were U.S. citizens.)

To the extent that the sample of people to be analyzed here is not representative of the national population, the results I report cannot be generalized to the nation as a whole. But it is not at all clear that one would want to generalize to the nation as a whole. Presidential primary elections take place, after all, in states. And no one supposes (or should suppose, at any rate) that the states that hold presidential primaries are representative of the 50. It is worth pointing out that the seven states analyzed here are not exactly like the other states, especially in the degree to which their populations are urban and suburban. But I do not believe that the demographic differences between these states and the others limit the usefulness of the results.

Of greater concern is the extent to which the respondents included in the analysis are representative of residents of the seven states. The format of the CPS sequence of questions about voting introduces some nonresponse bias in the measure of turnout in primaries. The question about primary turnout falls near the end of the sequence. It was not asked of people who responded "don't know" to the previous questions asking whether they had voted in the general election, whether they were registered to vote, whether they had ever voted in a national, state, or local election, and when the last time was that they had voted; it was also not asked of anyone who, for one reason or another, was not asked one of the previous questions in the sequence. There were numerous opportunities, in short, for respondents to be excluded or to exclude themselves from the question of whether they had voted in a primary. Primary voting was not ascertained for a total of 9.4 percent of the citizens in the seven sample states; another 2.6 percent said they did not know whether they had voted in a primary. This relatively large percentage who did not know whether they had voted in a primary is no doubt partly due to another shortcoming of the CPS for studying primary turnout: the survey was conducted in November, many months after the last primary election was over.

The respondents with missing turnout data are not drawn with equal probability from the entire sample. They are slightly younger than those for whom data are available; people over the age of 65, as some might expect, were slightly less likely than younger people to know the last time they voted. People with at least a college education were about 6 percentage points more likely than people with less than eight years of school to be asked and to answer the question about primary turnout. Men were about 3 percentage points less likely than women, blacks about 3 percentage points less likely than nonblacks, and the poorest about 3 percentage points less likely than the wealthiest to be asked and to give an answer to the question about primary turnout. (Again, these figures are for respondents who were U.S. citizens.) The sample of people whose primary voting may be analyzed, then, is a censored sample, for the respondents whose primary voting is known do not constitute a random sample of all respondents. Since the statistical technique I use to estimate the effects of demographic characteristics on turnout is not a linear one, there is no straightforward procedure to correct for the biased sample (Achen, 1986, p. 106). The fact that the sample to be analyzed is slightly more upscale than the entire seven-state sample will simply have to be borne in mind when assessing the results reported here. To maintain comparability across the multivariate analyses of registration, general-election turnout, and primary turnout, I excluded cases with missing data on any one of the three dependent variables from all three analyses.

Appendix B: Coding

Registration: Not registered = 0; Registered = 1.

General-election turnout and primary turnout: Did not vote = 0; Voted = 1.

Education: 0–4 years = 1; 5–7 years = 2; 8 years = 3; 9–11 years = 4; 12 years = 5; 13–15 years = 6; 16 years = 7; 17 years or more = 8.

Age: actual number of years up to 99.

Income: $0–4999 = 1; $5000–9999 = 2; $10,000–14,999 = 3; $15,000–19,999 = 4; $20,000–24,999 = 5; $25,000–49,999 = 6; $50,000 or more = 7.

Sex: Male = 0; Female = 1.

Race: White or other = 0; Black = 1.

Hispanicity: Other ethnicity = 0; Mexican-American, Chicano, Mexican or Mexicano, Puerto Rican, Cuban, Central or South American, or other Spanish = 1.

Length of time at current address: Less than 1 month = .083; 1–3 months = .167; 4–6 months = .417; 7–11 months = .75; 1–2 years = 1.5; 3–5 years = 4; 6–9 years = 7.5; 10 years or more = 10.

APPENDIX C   Logit Estimates of the Effects of Demographic Variables and Registration Closing Date on Registration, General-Election Turnout and Primary Election Turnout in Seven States with Concurrent 1976 Primary Elections

	1976 Current Population Survey[a]		
	Registration	General Election Turnout	Primary Election Turnout
Constant	-4.118 (.149)	-4.352 (.143)	-5.090 (.142)
Education	.133 (.040)	.121 (.038)	.275 (.034)
Education^2	.042 (.004)	.040 (.004)	.009 (.003)
Age	.093 (.004)	.103 (.003)	.104 (.003)
Age^2	-.001 (.000)	-.001 (.000)	-.001 (.000)
Income	.154 (.009)	.166 (.009)	.095 (.008)
Women	.074 (.024)	.075 (.023)	-.026 (.022)
Blacks	.323 (.043)	.211 (.040)	.285 (.039)
Hispanics	-.044 (.052)	-.138 (.051)	.058 (.053)
Length of Time at Residence	.038 (.013)	.051 (.013)	.070 (.012)
Closing Date	-.008 (.003)	-.013 (.003)	-.014 (.003)
Closing Date * Length at Residence	.002 (.000)	.002 (.000)	.001 (.000)
Model Likelihood Ratio Chi-Square:	7236	8204	7714
Percent of Cases Concordant:	73.2	75.8	76.5
Degrees of Freedom:		11	
Unweighted Cases:		25,777	

[a]Includes only U.S. citizens for whom complete demographic and voting information is available.

Note: Standard errors in parentheses.

Notes

My thanks to the State Data Program, the Survey Research Center, and the Department of Political Science of the University of California, Berkeley, for their support. Thanks also to Raymond Wolfinger, for his comments on an earlier draft.

1. In 1984 the Bureau of the Census tested the effects of using proxy responses on CPS estimates of the number of people who voted in the general election. A sample of the people whose voting and registration were reported by another household member was subsequently interviewed and asked the voting and registration questions directly. The Bureau found no evidence that proxy respondents systematically misreported the voting behavior of other household members (U.S. Bureau of the Census, 1986). The data provided by proxy therefore are included in this analysis.

2. The data on which this analysis relies were obtained through the State Data Program of the University of California, Berkeley, and were made available by the Inter-University Consortium for Political and Social Research. Neither those organizations nor the original collectors of the data bear any responsibility for the results reported here.

3. For an explanation of why I chose this particular set of states, see Appendix A. The CPS does not include questions about party affiliations. I cannot examine, therefore, turnout in Democratic and Republican primaries separately. Moreover, the analysis here must make a possibly restrictive assumption: the effects of demographic characteristics on primary turnout among Democrats and among Republicans must be assumed to be the same. I know of evidence to suggest that, other things being equal, this assumption is not correct. Given the dearth of individual-level data on turnout in primaries and the advantages of the CPS, however, I believe that the results reported here nevertheless may prove useful. A nod in the direction of the scholars who argue that party identification is endogenous to the voting decision may help to excuse my failure to take partisanship into account (e.g., Jackson, 1975; Page and Jones, 1979; Markus and Converse, 1979); with a little planning, after all, anyone may vote in either party's primary.

4. When the Census Bureau calculates general-election turnout from the CPS, as for the biennial Current Population Report on voting and registration, noncitizens and people who did not know whether they had voted and people who were not asked the question about turnout and people in sample households where no interviews were conducted are included—as nonvoters. The Bureau's most recent published argument for including noncitizens among the nonvoters is the following sentence: "Voting participation rates based on total population statistics are of sociological and political importance since they indicate the degree to which different population groups play a role in the electoral process" (U.S. Bureau of the Census, 1983, p. X). The Bureau's reason for failing to exclude missing data from the calculations is the following: "Nonrespondents and persons who reported that they did not know if they voted were included in the 'did not vote' class because of the general overreporting by respondents

in the sample" (U.S. Bureau of the Census, 1986, p. 86). Rather than assume that people whose turnout was not reported did not vote, I excluded them from the calculations on reported on Table 3.1 and throughout the analysis.

5. The five months that elapsed between the last of the 1976 presidential primary elections and the survey in November probably causes the CPS registration figures to be biased upward to some extent because of people who moved, not to mention those who died. The CPS asked respondents only whether they were registered to vote in the fall election, not whether they were registered to vote in the primary and not whether they were registered to vote at their current address. A substantial fraction of people who were registered to vote in November probably were not registered to vote in a primary. Data from the only National Election Study to ask respondents about registration both before and after the general election—the 1980 survey—show that 20 percent of those who said in September or October that they were not registered said in November or December that they were. People who had recently moved in November of 1976 comprise a group in the CPS for whom inferring registration in time for a primary is especially problematic. Sixteen percent of the citizens who lived in the seven states and whose primary voting was ascertained revealed that they had lived at their current address for more than one month but less than one year. Nearly all of those people would have been required to re-register in order to vote in a primary or in the November election (those who returned to their previous precincts and/or gave their old address at the polling place are the only exceptions). Yet 55 percent of them said they were registered. Since a presidential election took place between the time they moved and the date of the survey, many were no doubt prompted to re-register in September or October, and not for the primary.

6. I chose the closing date as the registration requirement to include because it previously has been found to be the requirement with the largest impact on turnout in a general election (Wolfinger and Rosenstone, 1980, p. 71). Moreover, the seven states in the sample were not very different from one another with respect to other registration arrangements. All seven purged the names of nonvoters from the registration rolls after two to four years, for example, and all seven allowed absentee registration. The number of days in advance of an election that one was required to register in the seven states, however, varied substantially, from 13 days in Ohio to 40 days in New Jersey. The data on registration arrangements are from Wolfinger and Rosenstone (1980, pp. 68–70). I do not know whether any of these arrangements were changed after the 1972 general election—the election for which the registration data were gathered— and before the 1976 primaries.

7. The coding schemes I employed are described in Appendix B. Only 25,777 respondents from the 1976 CPS sample were available for the multivariate analyses. Most of the respondents who were excluded were not citizens or their registration or turnout was not ascertained. The remainder were excluded because data on some of their demographic characteristics—in almost all cases, their family incomes—were missing.

8. I used logit to estimate the parameters of the model. The logit estimates are reported in Appendix C. Logit coefficients themselves are notoriously difficult

to interpret, because they do not describe effects in the metrics of the original variables. Figures that are easier to interpret describe the effects in terms of the percentage-point differences predicted by the logit models between a baseline group and each of the other groups defined by a particular explanatory variable, with the effects of all the other explanatory variables statistically controlled. The procedure I employed for calculating these estimates is similar to that described, in the context of probit analysis, by Wolfinger and Rosenstone (1980, appendix C).

9. Barbara Norrander (1982), using 1980 data, also found that education had a smaller impact on primary turnout than on general-election turnout.

10. Other research also has shown that blacks appear somewhat more likely to vote in general elections, at least in presidential elections, when the effects of other demographic variables are controlled (Olsen, 1970; Verba and Nie, 1972; Wolfinger and Rosenstone, 1980). People who are not black and not white—coded with whites in this analysis—make up less than 2 percent of the sample analyzed here, so their low rates of turnout are unlikely to be responsible for the reported difference between blacks and nonblacks.

11. It is worth pointing out again that noncitizens—who make up large portions of the Hispanic populations in California and Texas—are not included in this analysis.

12. These figures may overestimate the impact of age on primary turnout, as a by-product of the timing of the CPS survey, for the very low rates of primary turnout among young people may be partly artifactual. The CPS assessed the ages of respondents in mid-November, soon after the general election but months after the primaries. A substantial number of the respondents who were eighteen in November, and so were eligible to vote in the general election and to answer the question about primary voting, would not have been eighteen when their state held its primary. The CPS does not include information about date of birth, so such people cannot be distinguished. Nor does the question about primary turnout include a code for people who were eligible to vote in the general election but not in a primary. If such people were simply coded as not voting in a primary, the turnout rate of the youngest group is artificially reduced.

13. Angus Campbell (1966) used the term "core voters" to refer to people who voted both in presidential and in mid-term elections.

14. The multivariate analysis suggests the same substantive interpretation. The evidence is easier to see, however, in the bivariate tables. Moreover, those tables reveal the "floor effect," while the logit analysis assumes one.

15. The unrepresentativeness of general-election voters in 1972 is described in Wolfinger and Rosenstone (1980, pp. 104–108). The representativeness of presidential primary voters relative to general-election voters has been noted by Kritzer (1980) with regard to the 1972 elections and by Rubin (1980) with regard to the 1976 elections. Contrary to the results I report here, Polsby (1983, pp. 158–159) found that, among Democrats in 1976, primary voters nationwide were not representative of general-election voters. Norrander (1986) compared 1980 general-election voters who did and did not vote in the primaries. Ranney

and Epstein (1966) found that demographic differences between, on the one hand, people who voted in the 1964 Wisconsin gubernatorial primary and general elections and, on the other, people who voted in the general election but not the primary were much like differences typically found between general-election voters and nonvoters. Ranney (1968) found that the voters in the 1966 Wisconsin gubernatorial primary were unrepresentative of the nonvoters with respect to demographic characteristics typically found to be related to turnout in general elections. He suggested that "primary voters are unrepresentative of primary non-voters in about the same respects in which general election voters are unrepresentative of general election non-voters" (p. 231). And DiNitto and Smithers (1972) found no significant demographic differences between residents of Amsterdam, New York who voted in the congressional primary of 1970 and those who voted in the subsequent general election.

16. Hispanics, because they make up a very small portion of the voting-age citizens, were more severely underrepresented than the percentage-point difference indicates. Dividing the percentage of primary voters who were Hispanic by the percentage of citizens who were Hispanic shows that Hispanics' share of the primary electorate was just 69 percent of their share of voting-age citizens. Blacks' share of the primary electorate was 96 percent of their share of voting-age citizens.

17. The logit estimates appear in Appendix C. The fact that only seven states are included in this analysis limits the sample variation in closing dates. In technical terms, the sample distribution of closing dates is truncated, since none of the seven states had a closing date of less than 13 days or more than 40 days. It is worth noting, then, that when I estimated the impact of closing dates on general-election turnout using these data and a model ignoring any interaction between the closing date and residential mobility, I obtained an estimate exactly the same as that reported by Wolfinger and Rosenstone (1980, appendix F). Their 1972 sample included all 50 states, with a much wider range of closing dates.

18. Of course, the results for the effects of closing dates assume that none of the other ways in which the seven sample states differ is correlated with their closing dates. I have no reason to expect any such correlation, but some such correlation is certainly possible. With only seven states to analyze, my options in controlling for other state-level factors were severely limited.

19. See note 5.

20. Some of the people who said in November that they had lived at the same address for less than one month could not have voted in the state's primary, since they did not live in the state. Not many of the movers fall into this category, however, since 83 percent of all moves are within the same state (Squire, Wolfinger, and Glass, 1987, p. 57). The CPS does not include information about the state from which movers moved.

21. The parameter estimates on which these calculations are based appear in Appendix C. The method used to make the calculations is described in Wolfinger and Rosenstone (1980, pp. 139–140). As they note, the composition of the projected groups cannot be compared directly with the composition of

the actual electorate or the composition of the population of citizens (as described in the first four columns of Table 3.4), because those differences would be due not only to the projected probabilities but also to errors in prediction.

22. The seven were not, however, much different from the rest of the nation with respect to the demographic variables that were part of the analysis. See Appendix A.

23. I should add that I have not been able to include among the independent variables examined here the numerous other state-level variables that others have found to influence primary turnout—the rules governing the primary, the characteristics of the campaign, and the like. Given turnout data for seven states, the degrees of freedom were few.

References

Achen, Christopher H. 1986. *The Statistical Analysis of Quasi-Experiments.* Berkeley: University of California Press.

Aldrich, John H. 1980. *Before the Convention: Strategies and Choices in Presidential Nomination Campaigns.* Chicago: University of Chicago Press.

Brody, Richard A. 1978. The Puzzle of Political Participation in America. In Anthony King, ed., *The New American Political System.* Washington, DC: American Enterprise Institute.

Campbell, Angus. 1966. Surge and Decline: A Study of Electoral Change. In Angus Campbell, Philip E. Converse, Warren E. Miller, and Donald E. Stokes. *Elections and the Political Order.* New York: Wiley.

——, Philip E. Converse, Warren E. Miller, and Donald E. Stokes. 1960. *The American Voter.* New York: Wiley.

Citrin, Jack. 1978. The Alienated Voter. *Taxing and Spending.* October, pp. 1–7.

Crotty, William, and John S. Jackson III. 1985. *Presidential Primaries and Nominations.* Washington, DC: Congressional Quarterly Press.

Davis, James. 1980. *Presidential Primaries: Road to the White House.* Westport, Conn.: Greenwood Press.

DiNitto, Andrew, and William Smithers. 1972. The Representativeness of the Direct Primary. *Polity,* 5:209–24.

Green, Donald Philip. 1985. Toward a General Theory of Self-Interest Effects. Unpublished manuscript. Survey Research Center, University of California, Berkeley.

Gurian, Paul-Henri. 1986. Resource Allocation Strategies in Presidential Nomination Campaigns. *American Journal of Political Science,* 30:802–21.

Hagen, Michael G. 1988. Measuring Voter Registration and Turnout. Survey Research Center Working Paper. University of California, Berkeley.

Jackson, John E. 1975. Issues, Party Choices, and Presidential Votes. *American Journal of Political Science,* 19:161–85.

Kelley, Jr., Stanley, Richard E. Ayres, and William G. Bowen. 1967. Registration and Voting: Putting First Things First. *American Political Science Review,* 61:359–79.

Key, V.O. 1949. *Southern Politics.* New York: Knopf.

──────. 1956. *American State Politics: An Introduction.* New York: Knopf.

Kim, Jae-On, John R. Petrocik, and Stephen N. Enokson. 1975. Voter Turnout among the American States: Systemic and Individual Components. *American Political Science Review,* 69:107–23.

Kritzer, Herbert M. 1980. The Representativeness of the 1972 Presidential Primaries. In William Crotty, ed., *The Party Symbol.* San Francisco: W.H. Freeman.

Lengle, James I. 1980. Demographic Representation in California's 1972 and 1968 Democratic Presidential Primaries. In James I. Lengle and Byron E. Shafer, eds., *Presidential Politics.* New York: St. Martin's Press.

──────. 1981. *Representation and Presidential Primaries: The Democratic Party in the Post-Reform Era.* Westport, Conn.: Greenwood Press.

Markus, Gregory B., and Philip E. Converse. 1979. A Dynamic Simultaneous Equation Model of Electoral Choice. *American Political Science Review,* 73:1055–70.

Moran, Jack, and Mark Fenster. 1982. Voter Turnout in Presidential Primaries: A Diachronic Analysis. *American Politics Quarterly,* 10:453–76.

Morris, William D., and Otto A. Davis. 1975. The Sport of Kings: Turnout in Presidential Preference Primaries. Presented at the annual meeting of the American Political Science Association, San Francisco.

Norrander, Barbara. 1982. Determinants of Presidential Primary Participation: A Comparison to General Election Turnout. Presented at the annual meeting of the Midwest Political Science Association, Milwaukee, Wisconsin.

──────. 1986. Selective Participation: Presidential Primary Voters as a Subset of General Election Votes. *American Politics Quarterly,* 14:35–53.

──────, and Gregg W. Smith. 1985. Type of Contest, Candidate Strategy, and Turnout in Presidential Primaries. *American Politics Quarterly,* 13:28–50.

Olsen, Marvin E. 1970. Social and Political Participation of Blacks. *American Sociological Review,* 35:682–97.

Page, Benjamin I., and Calvin C. Jones. 1979. Reciprocal Effects of Policy Preferences, Party Loyalties, and the Vote. *American Political Science Review,* 73:1071–90.

Pitkin, Hanna Fenichel. 1967. *The Concept of Representation.* Berkeley: University of California Press.

Polsby, Nelson W. 1983. *Consequences of Party Reform.* New York: Oxford University Press.

Ranney, Austin. 1968. The Representativeness of Primary Elections. *Midwest Journal of Political Science,* 12:224–38.

──────. 1972. Turnout and Representation in Presidential Primary Elections. *American Political Science Review,* 66:21–37.

──────. 1977. *Participation in American Presidential Nominations, 1976.* Washington, DC: American Enterprise Institute for Public Policy Research.

──────. ed., 1981. *The American Elections of 1980.* Washington, DC: American Enterprise Institute.

──────. ed., 1985. *The American Elections of 1984.* Durham, N.C.: Duke University Press.

_____, and Leon Epstein. 1966. The Two Electorates: Voters and Non-Voters in a Wisconsin Primary. *Journal of Politics*, 28:598–616.

Rosenstone, Steven J., and Raymond E. Wolfinger. 1978. The Effect of Registration Laws on Voter Turnout. *American Political Science Review*, 72:22–45.

Rothenberg, Lawrence S., and Richard A. Brody. 1988. Participation in Presidential Primaries. *Western Political Quarterly*, 41:253–71.

Rubin, Richard L. 1980. Presidential Primaries: Continuities, Dimensions of Change, and Political Implications. In William Crotty, ed., *The Party Symbol*. San Francisco: W.H. Freeman.

Schier, Steven E. 1982. Turnout Choice in Presidential Nominations: A Case Study. *American Politics Quarterly*, 10:231–45.

Squire, Peverill, Raymond E. Wolfinger, and David P. Glass. 1987. Residential Mobility and Voter Turnout. *American Political Science Review*, 81:45–65.

U.S. Bureau of the Census. 1983. Voting and Registration in the Election of November 1982. *Current Population Reports*, Series P–20, No. 383. Washington, DC: U.S. Government Printing Office.

_____. 1986. Voting and Registration in the Election of November 1984. *Current Population Reports*, Series P–20, No. 405. Washington, DC: U.S. Government Printing Office.

Verba, Sidney, and Norman H. Nie. 1972. *Participation in America*. New York: Harper and Row.

Wolfinger, Raymond E., and Steven J. Rosenstone. 1980. *Who Votes?* New Haven, CT: Yale University Press.

Zeidenstein, Harvey. 1970. Presidential Primaries: Reflection of the People's Choice? *Journal of Politics*, 32:856–74.

4

Is Iowa News?

Henry E. Brady

What's News?

The Rules of Media Coverage. You're a news editor. The presidential election is one of the biggest stories of the year. How do you cover it? What's news?

First things first. Iowa is the first caucus state and New Hampshire the first primary state. They will affect all the caucuses and primaries which follow them. They deserve extensive coverage.

Second, when the stakes are bigger, the news is bigger. War and peace, death and taxes, these things are news. For the nominating process, the stakes are big in two cases: when the competition is intense and when big blocks of delegates are up for grabs. Competition is most intense at the beginning of the nomination process. A single misstep can ruin a campaign. Many are the unremembered candidates who have found their money and their desire evaporating after Iowa and New Hampshire.

Third, candidates play to win, and the system provides the simple scoring rule of delegates won. Like the Dow-Jones, economic indicators, the size of the budget, and presidential popularity, the "horse-race" of the nomination process is a natural news story. Who's winning and who's losing delegates deserves a great deal of attention.

Fourth, the unexpected, like a man biting a dog, is news. In political campaigns, expectations are formed about character and behavior, and deviations from these expectations, such as Gary Hart's monkey business, are news. Yet, even when actual behavior confounds expectations in surprising ways, it is often hard to be sure of the event's newsworthiness. The complexity of our moral standards, for example, makes even Gary Hart's dalliance with Donna Rice or Ronald Reagan's involvement in the Iran-Contra affair a matter of confusion and uncertainty. The media may still press these issues, but their footing is often unsure.

It is far easier to establish the newsworthiness of horse-race events. Despite Edmund Muskie's protestations, most reporters and readers agreed with David Broder's January, 1972, column in which he set the standard for Muskie's performance in New Hampshire: "As the acknowledged front runner and a resident of the neighboring state, Muskie will have to win the support of at least half the New Hampshire Democrats in order to claim a victory." Moreover, when the returns came in, it was a simple arithmetical exercise to judge whether or not Muskie met this standard. Moral truth, absent the advice of Allan Bloom, may be an elusive basis for newsworthiness, but arithmetic offers a solid foundation for judging news.

Fifth, whatever else, there must be a "story." Journalists are taught to get the story, to write the story, and to sell the story. A good news story is simple and dramatic. There must be a protagonist and an antagonist. There can be some other characters, but not too many. They should serve only as comic relief, human interest, or devices to further the plot. Simplicity is the key. The front-runner is the obvious protagonist. The challenger is the antagonist. This can be the "insurgent" who breaks with his party, the "outsider" who lacks establishment credentials, the "ideologue" who challenges the center of the party, the "young turk" who brings new ideas to his elders, or the "old war-horse" who returns after many a campaign.

The Results of Media Coverage. By this reckoning, it is no surprise that the nominating process has brought us these stories over the last twenty years:

- Gene McCarthy in New Hampshire in 1968—The "insurgent" within his party making a brave showing against his party's president, Lyndon Johnson.
- George McGovern in Iowa and New Hampshire in 1972—The "outsider" making a strong bid against the insider's candidate, Edmund Muskie.
- Ronald Reagan in Iowa and New Hampshire in 1976—The "ideologue" challenging the center of the party.
- Gary Hart in Iowa in 1984—The "young turk" bringing new ideas into a somewhat tired party led by Walter Mondale.

With just a good showing in Iowa or New Hampshire, these candidates had a substantial impact on their party's nomination process: McCarthy's success led to Johnson's withdrawal from the presidential race, McGovern eventually garnered the nomination, Reagan revealed Ford's weakness and set the stage for his own successful nomination in 1980, and Hart almost won the nomination from the heavily favored Walter Mondale.

Yet, neither McCarthy, McGovern, Reagan, nor Hart won the events described above. What they did do was to perform better than expected while their chief rivals did worse. What they provided was a dramatic story for the press. What they accomplished was to set the nomination campaign on a new course.

Jimmy Carter's Iowa "win" (behind "uncommitted") in 1976 certainly set his campaign on a new course. Carter's victory in Iowa propelled him to victory in New Hampshire and on to the Democratic nomination. In 1980, Iowa again helped Carter when he repulsed a strong challenge from Edward Kennedy by winning in Iowa and then in New Hampshire.

Iowa and New Hampshire are news. What about Iowa alone? One could argue, on the one hand, that New Hampshire has "chosen" more presidential nominees than Iowa. From 1968 to 1988, the winners of the New Hampshire Republican primary (Nixon twice, Ford, Reagan twice, and Bush) have won the nomination. On the Democratic side, the winners in New Hampshire in 1976, 1980, and 1988 (Carter twice and Dukakis once) won the nomination. In 1972 and 1984, the second place finishers (McGovern and Mondale) won the nomination. New Hampshire, then, has "chosen" the party's nominees nine out of twelve times since 1968. Iowa, on the other hand, has only "chosen" the nominee four out of eight times since 1972.[1] In fact, in two cases, Iowa has been more of a detour than the road to the nomination. In 1980, George Bush's hopes were raised by his victory in Iowa only to be dashed by Ronald Reagan's convincing victory in New Hampshire. In 1988, Bob Dole's campaign followed the same dead-end route.

These stories and statistics, however, understate Iowa's influence. New Hampshire has a much better record of choosing the nominee precisely because Iowa precedes it. Iowa has been important in almost every quadrennium because its caucuses have defined the field of contenders either by catapulting newcomers like McGovern, Carter, and Hart to the forefront and dashing the hopes of other hopefuls or by providing a clear-cut sense of the vulnerabilities of incumbents such as Ford in 1976 and Carter in 1980.

The Media's Decision Rules

Our story so far may be a good news story: Iowa, it seems, is news. Our explanation for this seems plausible, but does it agree with the facts? Do the news media really act as we have claimed? Do their actions really change the course of the nomination process? Is this good or bad? When all is said and done, should Iowa be news?

The UPI Data-Set. To learn about the media's decision rules, we undertook a content analysis of every United Press International (UPI) story on one of the eight Democratic candidates from January 1, 1984, to July 31, 1984.[2] Each story was broken up into story parts which involved a unified discussion of a "candidate," on a particular "subject," drawing from a particular "base" of information. Two versions of the "dateline" for the story were also coded. In one version, the "place" from which the reporter filed the story was coded along with the "time" it was reported. In another version, a coder noted whether any "location" was mentioned in each story part.

The story parts were classified into six major subjects. These were chosen so as to answer the basic questions which might occur to a journalist or a newspaper reader. The major subjects and their subtopics along with the question motivating each category are listed below:

1. *Is the candidate winning?* This includes all story parts on the "potential or actual success of the candidate" including viability, electability, campaign organization, and fund raising abilities.
2. *Who supports the candidate?* All parts on "sources of support or opposition" including individuals (e.g., Tip O'Neill), organized groups (AFL-CIO, Sierra Club), and unorganized groups (Hispanics, environmentalists).
3. *What is the candidate like?* Parts on "candidate issues" including the candidate's experience (record of public service, previous offices held), leadership ability (intelligence, knowledge, strength, decisiveness, self-confidence), personal qualities (honesty, sincerity, integrity, likability, appearance, health), and human interest (news about the candidate's wife, children, parents, childhood, or background).
4. *What does the candidate stand for?* Parts on "issues of government policy" including social, economic, defense, government operations, and all other policy areas.
5. *What does the candidate say about his opponents?* All "comments about other candidates" including Ronald Reagan, the eight Democrats, the Republican party generally, or general comments about the other Democratic candidates.
6. *What other events have involved the candidate?* All "other events" including debates, campaign appearances, social events, non-campaign public events, non-campaign private events.

For each type of story (with one exception), we asked our coders to judge on a five point scale "the overall impression of the candidate conveyed by the discussion in this part of the story." This was probably the most difficult judgment our coders had to make (although some felt that determining the basis was even harder), but it is very important for much of the following analysis. When making these judgments, we asked our coders to think like an average newspaper reader. Through repeated discussion sessions, we felt that we reached some consensus on how to do this. The one exception occurred when the story was about one candidate commenting about another. In that case, we asked the coders to tell us what the candidate's evaluation was of the subject of his comments.

Iowa and New Hampshire as News. Did our UPI journalists place more emphasis upon Iowa and New Hampshire than other states because they came first in the nomination process? To answer this question, we constructed two different measures of reporting about primaries and caucuses. One measure called "place" simply took the UPI dateline attached to each story and classified it as one of the fifty states, the District of Columbia, or some foreign locale. Another measure called "location" was coded by reading each story part and determining whether it referred to a state in connection with the campaign. The following analyses are based upon the "place" measure, but almost identical results were obtained with the "location" measure.

Casual observation suggests that most of the coverage of primary and caucus events is concentrated near the events themselves. We would expect to find much more coverage of an event three days before or after it occurs than thirty days before or after. To check this hypothesis, we took each story-part with a state as a dateline and classified it according to the number of days ("event-days") it appeared before or after the primary or caucus event in that state. Then we summed the number of lines of coverage of a particular type of event, say primaries, that appeared on each event day. For example, for all primary states, we summed up the number of lines of coverage that occurred in each of them on the fortieth (thirty-ninth, . . . , third, etc.) day before the primary in each state. Figure 4.1a plots a smoothed version of the number of lines of coverage by the number of days before and after each primary, and Figure 4.1b plots the same smoothed measure by days before and after the caucuses.[3] These plots have the same horizontal scale of "event-days," but different vertical scales so that Figure 4.1a for primaries has three times as many lines per division as Figure 4.1b for caucuses. The daily average values are indicated by the integer "1" except when more than one value occurs at the same location in which case the integer represents the number of superimposed values.

There are two significant findings from this analysis. First of all, the shape of coverage is similar for both primaries and caucuses. As indicated by the dashed lines, most of the coverage occurs within thirty days before the event and a week after the event. The only exception occurs about 50 days before the primaries where there appears to be some

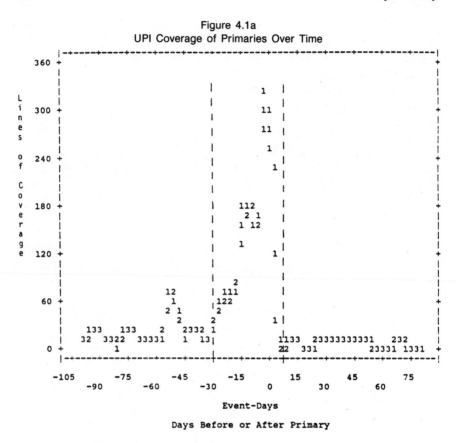

Figure 4.1a
UPI Coverage of Primaries Over Time

Source: Brady-Hagen UPI Data.

significant coverage. This is almost entirely articles about New Hampshire that appeared in early January, 1984. This suggests that a good summary measure of coverage is the number of lines devoted to a particular event between one month before it occurs and one week after it has happened. These 37 days are more than Andy Warhol's fifteen minutes of media fame, but they have the same ephemeral character. Each event is important in anticipation and important for a few days after its occurrence, but then the media go on to the next event with barely a second thought.

The second major finding is that primaries receive much more coverage than caucuses, and the coverage is more drawn out—the curve is thicker in its midsection for primaries than it is for caucuses. A clear indicator of the relative importance of the two types of events is the average number of lines of coverage for each—forty-nine for caucus states and

Figure 4.1b
UPI Coverage of Caucuses Over Time

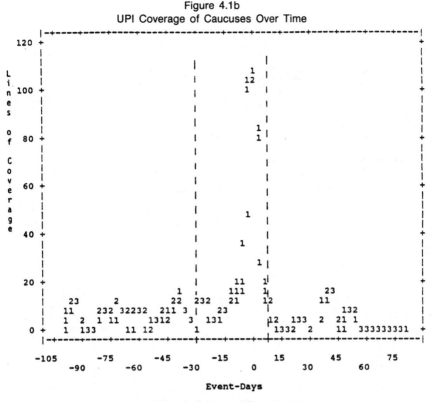

Event-Days

Days Before or After Caucus

Source: Brady-Hagen UPI Data.

215 for primary states. Among the caucus states, Texas received the most coverage, 252 lines, but Iowa, with half the number of delegates, was close with 234 lines of coverage. Among the primary states, California (513 lines), Georgia (600 lines), New York (540 lines), and Florida (482 lines) received more coverage than New Hampshire, but California had about 16 times as many delegates, Georgia had almost four times the delegates, New York had thirteen times as many, and Florida had more than six times as many. Moreover, Georgia and Florida were two of the "Super Tuesday" states which came early in the nomination process, and Georgia was considered a "must-win" state for Walter Mondale after his loss to Gary Hart in New Hampshire.

These specific cases suggest that three things determine media coverage: the type of event with caucuses receiving less coverage than primaries, the number of delegates up for grabs in the state, and the timing of

TABLE 4.1   Determinants of State Coverage

	Primaries Beta / (Std. Error)	Caucuses Beta / (Std. Error)
First States		
Iowa	--------	243.4** (63.1)
New Hampshire	367.7* (161.9)	--------
Systematic Factors		
Delegates from State	1.6*** (.3)	.46 (.29)
Date of Event	-1.5 (1.0)	1.4 (.8)
Constant	135.4 (154.8)	114.0 (70.0)
R^2	.65	.57

* < .05
** < .01
*** < .001

the event. Simple plots of the lines of coverage versus the number of delegates and the timing of the event suggest that these are important variables. One other variable may have an effect on coverage. The number of primaries and caucuses on a particular day may focus the media's attention.

Table 4.1 presents the results of separate regression runs for primaries and caucuses which incorporate these variables. The number of lines of coverage for a state in the month before and the week after the state's selection of delegates is the dependent variable, and the explanatory variables include the number of delegates from the state, the number of competing events, the date of the event (numbered consecutively from January 1st), and separate variables for the first two events, Iowa and New Hampshire.

The equation for caucuses is disappointing. None of the variables, except the dummy variable for Iowa, is significant. The importance of Iowa is not surprising based upon the raw linecounts. All but three of the 23 caucus states received fewer than 76 lines of coverage and ten received fewer than ten lines. The three with more than 76 lines of

Figure 4.2
Lines of Coverage by Subject Matter (in Percent)

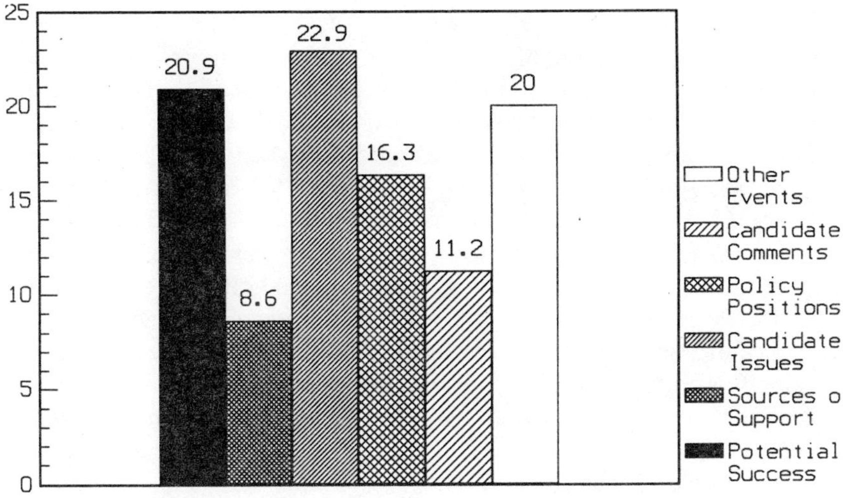

coverage are Texas (252 lines), which has more than three times as many delegates as Iowa, Arkansas (177 lines), and, of course, Iowa.

The equation for the primaries is more informative. Clearly the number of delegates has an important impact on coverage for the primary states. For these states, each additional delegate leads to about one and one-half additional lines of coverage. Since the range of lines of coverage is about the same as the range of delegates, this is a substantively important result. There seems to be no statistical evidence for an effect from the number of events on a given day, and there is no evidence for the impact of the date of the primary except, of course, for New Hampshire. The equation provides a striking confirmation of New Hampshire's importance. Even though it has a small number of delegates and it is a solitary event, it is accorded exceptional coverage—368 more lines of coverage than one would expect![4]

Being first matters. Having delegates matters.

The Emphasis on the Horse-Race. Do the media emphasize the horse-race? Not entirely by any means. Figure 4.2 indicates that less than one-fifth of the coverage could be called "horse-race" coverage. A little less than a tenth deals with sources of support; another fifth focuses on the character of the candidates. A sixth discusses their policy positions, and a little over a tenth reports candidate's comments about each other. Finally, the remaining fifth describes various events of the campaigns.

It would seem unfair to argue that this pattern of coverage shows that the UPI was preoccupied with the horse-race. Over the course of the campaign, the UPI, at least, was not gripped by the need to report who was ahead and who was behind. Yet, the UPI emphasized the horse-race at some crucial moments, and its horse-race coverage was more evaluative than most of its reporting. Consider Figure 4.3. Viability coverage (just one component of those stories about the candidates' potential success) began to build quickly around Iowa (February 20th) and New Hampshire (February 28th), and it peaked on Super Tuesday (March 13th). Indeed, at this point it equalled the combined coverage on candidate issues and policy issues.

Moreover, Table 4.2 demonstrates that viability coverage is one of the most evaluative forms of reporting. The last two columns of this table present two measures of the extremity of coverage. Of the six major categories in this table, three of them, candidate issues, policy positions, and other events, have a large percentage (fewer than 36 percent) of lines with zero evaluations and a small percentage (fewer than 15 percent) of lines with extreme evaluations of two or minus two on the five point evaluation scale. When covering issues or simply campaign events, the media tend to be modest in their evaluations.

The UPI was much more evaluative in its coverage of the three remaining categories. Those stories on potential success are reports of the success or failure of each candidate's army in the battle for the nomination—who is viable, electable, well-organized, and well-funded, and who is not. There is probably some information on the character and quality of the candidates in these reports, but they are mostly just about the horse-race. The other two categories, stories on candidates' comments about one another and sources of support, deal with the rhetoric and diplomacy which go on behind the battle. Unlike the reports of the battle itself which contain little direct information about the moral and intellectual standing of the candidates, these stories do provide some substantive information, but their major quality is that they provide more texture to the overall horse-race.

In summary, the UPI presented a substantial amount of information about the candidates and their policy positions, but there was also a significant amount of coverage of the horse-race. Moreover, this coverage peaked at the beginning of the nominating process, and it tended to be highly evaluative.

Emphasizing the Unexpected. If the media find it easier to identify and explain surprises in the horse-race than in other aspects of the campaign, then we would expect to find that coverage of the candidates would turn on their wins and losses more than on anything else. Furthermore, we would expect that much of this coverage would be highly evaluative reports about viability. Figure 4.4 shows how the total lines of coverage

Figure 4.3
UPI Coverage of Four Subject Areas, by Week

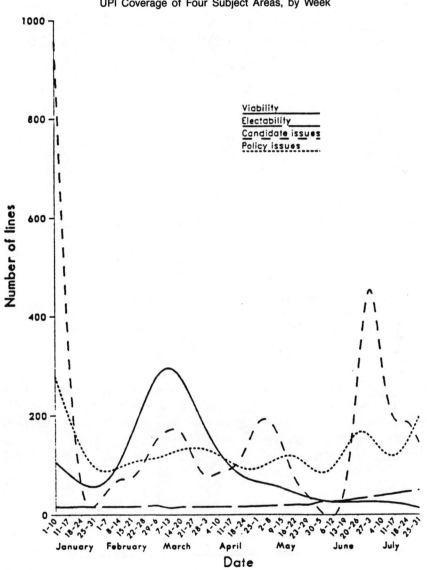

TABLE 4.2   Determinants of State Coverage

Subjects	Number of Lines	Average Evaluation	% of Lines with Zero Evaluation	% of Extreme Evaluations
Potential Success	5044	.187	19.5	21.0
Viability	3017	.324	16.8	25.2
Electability	736	-.132	20.7	16.4
Campaign Org.	914	.079	39.3	9.0
Funding	377	-.103	9.3	25.7
Sources of Support	2073	.500	13.4	17.8
Candidate Issues	5540	.319	36.2	15.1
Experience	185	.032	29.2	22.2
Leadership	1784	.715	8.9	33.6
Personal Qual.	853	-.101	23.3	19.0
Human Interest	2718	.211	58.7	1.2
Policy Positions	3946	.127	67.4	3.9
Candidate Comments	2705	-.928	15.7	31.7
About Jackson	381	.108	17.1	21.8
About Others	2324	-1.099	15.4	32.5
Other Events	4840	.388	57.5	5.4
Campaign App.	2000	.283	68.2	2.8
Public Events	2159	.536	41.2	9.4
All Other	681	.225	77.5	0
Totals	24,148	.148	38.1	14.6

for each candidate changed over time, and Figure 4.5 presents weekly changes in UPI evaluations of viability.

Figure 4.4 tells a very clear story. For John Glenn, Gary Hart, and Walter Mondale, the outcomes of the primaries and caucuses determined the number of lines of coverage they received. Hart received little coverage before he took second in Iowa, but then he quickly surpassed both Glenn and Mondale until Mondale's resurgence in April with wins in the Wisconsin caucuses and the Pennsylvania primary. As Super Tuesday approached, coverage for all three candidates increased, but Glenn's poor showings in Iowa and New Hampshire translated into a much smaller increase. With his failure to come back on Super Tuesday, Glenn's coverage quickly faded to nothing. Finally, after his win in New Jersey on June 5th, Walter Mondale's coverage increased dramatically as the Democratic Convention approached.

Figure 4.5 shows how the evaluative tone of the viability coverage for Glenn, Hart, and Mondale changed dramatically as the events of the campaign unfolded. One first notices that Hart and Glenn's viability coverage were mirror images of one another from Iowa until Glenn's withdrawal just before the Illinois primary. Closer inspection reveals

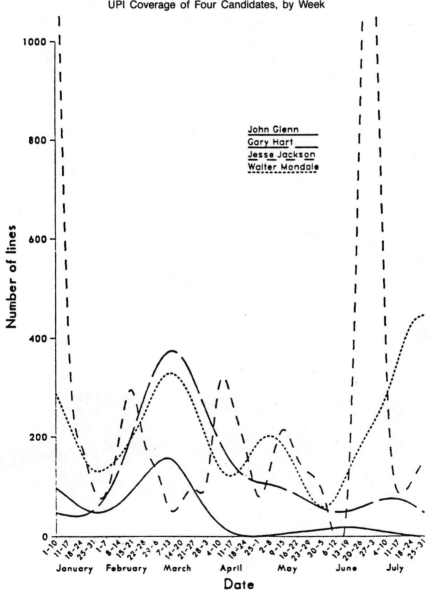

Figure 4.4
UPI Coverage of Four Candidates, by Week

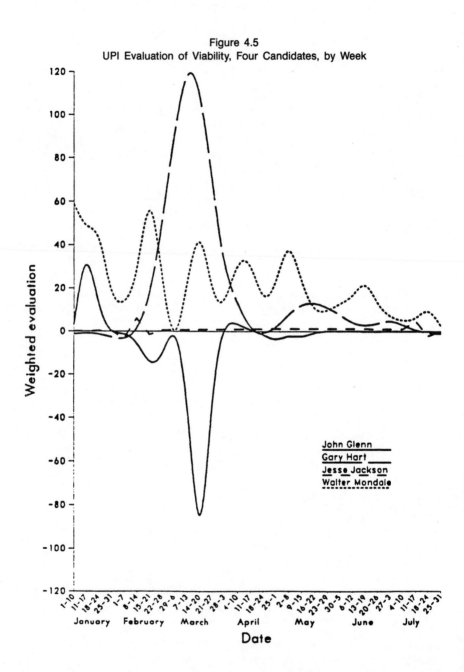

Figure 4.5
UPI Evaluation of Viability, Four Candidates, by Week

that the Mondale and Hart coverage were also highly negatively correlated from Iowa onwards. Indeed, the correlation between normalized measures of the Mondale and Hart evaluations is $-.86$ from Iowa until the end of July. First Mondale and Glenn and then Mondale and Hart served as the central characters of the media's ongoing story about the nomination process. Figure 4.5 shows that when one of these characters had a success or failure, the media quickly provided a clear-cut evaluation of this turn in the plot, and Figure 4.4 shows that they provided copious coverage of this new development.

Iowa and its aftermath provides a striking example of the media's coverage after an important event. As shown on Figure 4.6, in the week before Iowa, Mondale received 50 percent of the total UPI coverage for Glenn, Hart, and Mondale. Hart only received 27 percent. In the Iowa caucuses, Mondale received 45 percent of the preference votes, Hart took a distant second with 15 percent, and Glenn was fifth with 5 percent. George McGovern took third with 13 percent of the preference votes. Despite the fact that he finished second and only barely beat George McGovern, Hart received 52 percent of the UPI coverage allocated to Glenn, Hart, and Mondale in the week after Iowa. George McGovern received virtually no coverage. Hart was the story because he exceeded expectations.

Telling a Simple Story. But why was Hart the whole story? Why wasn't George McGovern's surprisingly strong showing in Iowa featured by the media? McGovern's staffers have told me that they went to bed on Monday, February 20th believing that McGovern's performance would be a major story. McGovern had run a Quixotic issue-oriented campaign. He had been considered a loser after his defeat by Nixon in the 1972 campaign. Iowa seemed to show that the "old war horse" had some life left in him. The media, however, disagreed. Why?

Maybe the media discounted McGovern's third place showing in Iowa because South Dakota is nearby. Or maybe they didn't think he could really win the nomination because of his past failures. Our answer must be speculative, but we suspect that the media acted as they did because they wanted a simple and fresh story. Hart may have taken second by only the slimmest of margins, but he was still in second place, and he was new. He was a good story.

Jesse Jackson provides another example of a good story. The coverage he received was remarkably different from that of Glenn, Hart, or Mondale. It was not driven by the horse-race. Rather, it was the result of two major factors. First there were his diplomatic successes and campaign gaffes such as his trip to Syria in late December, 1983 to rescue a captured American airman and his comment about "Hymie-town" which produced a stir in early April. These events show up

Figure 4.6
Media Coverage and Results
Iowa, 1984

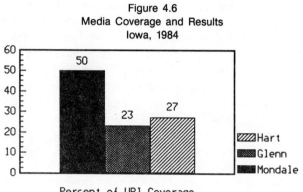

Percent of UPI Coverage
Week before Iowa

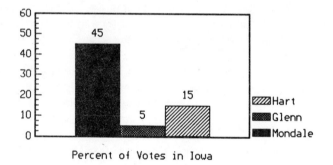

Percent of Votes in Iowa

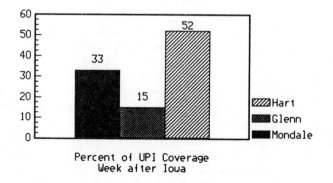

Percent of UPI Coverage
Week after Iowa

clearly in Figure 4.4, and they indicate that under some conditions the media will find the unexpected in places others than the ups and downs of the horse-race. Second, Jackson provided the human interest in campaign of 1984. He was not considered viable, and his weighted viability coverage on Figure 4.5 is virtually nil. Instead, he was a useful minor character who, as indicated by Figure 4.4, provided copy when the scheduled events of the campaign failed to provide any drama.

Jackson provided human interest. This shows up in the types of stories written about Jackson. Figures 4.7a and 4.7b show that the profile of Jackson coverage was quite different than the more typical profile of Hart coverage. Whereas Glenn, Hart, and Mondale all had profiles identical to Figure 4.7a, Jackson had a profile with much less discussion of his potential success, and much more discussion of other events. When the campaign got dull, editors asked for Jesse Jackson stories.

Reprise: The Rules of Media Coverage. The rules we proposed at the beginning of this paper are not just a caricature of media behavior. Because they come first, Iowa and New Hampshire do receive an exceptional amount of coverage. Because it is easy to follow, the horse-race is emphasized by the media, especially at the beginning of the nomination process. For the major candidates, a great deal of coverage turns on expectations and surprises in caucus and primary performances. Finally, the media try to tell a simple story with a protagonist, antagonist, and possibly a minor figure for human interest.

Individual Responses to the Media

This is all very well, but do the reports in the media affect voter behavior? Do citizens follow the media's lead and act in response to it? It would require a very lengthy paper to answer these questions completely. Rather than try, we shall provide some evidence that citizens' beliefs about the candidates do change over time and that the media are probably responsible for at least some of this change. In other work (Brady and Johnston, 1987), we have shown that these beliefs, in turn, affect behavior.

We can chart changes in citizens' beliefs in 1984 because we are lucky enough to have some remarkably useful data about the American electorate. In 1984, the American National Election Studies (NES) designed a weekly "rolling cross-section" which interviewed a random sample of about sixty-five Americans every week from January 11, 1984 to November 30, 1984. During this time, many questions about the characteristics of candidates and the characteristics of individual respondents were repeated from week to week. With these data we can study, for the first time, the evolution of the beliefs and attitudes of the American electorate as

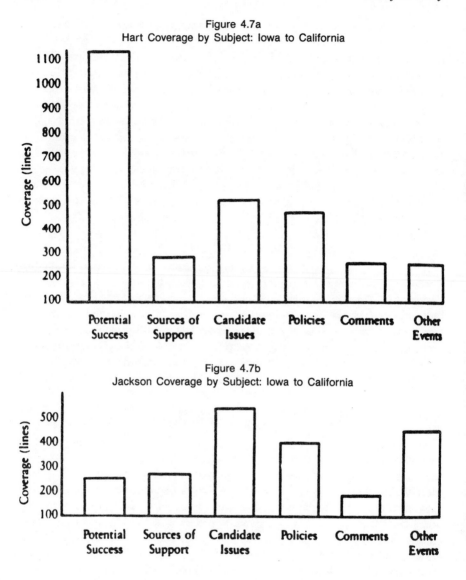

Figure 4.7a
Hart Coverage by Subject: Iowa to California

Figure 4.7b
Jackson Coverage by Subject: Iowa to California

the primary season progressed. These data, however, do have one significant limitation: They are samples of the national electorate and not the state electorates that actually voted in the primaries. Nevertheless, they do provide us with a wealth of information about how peoples' perceptions of the candidates changed over the course of the nomination process. We shall be especially interested in two types of perceptions: Assessments of candidates' traits and assessments of their chances of winning the nomination. We have argued elsewhere (Brady and Johnston, 1987; Brady and Hagen, 1986) that a good nomination process should provide citizens with information about candidates' traits but that viability assessments provide a less substantive and important kind of information. It is worth knowing whether voters learn more about traits or about viability.

Changing Impressions of Traits. At what point, if ever, do impressions become crystallized? Indeed, what is a crystallized impression? For us, a firm impression will generally have two characteristics: It will be relatively "distinct" or differentiated so that it will involve a recognition of some strengths and some weaknesses of the candidate. It will also be relatively "stable" so that the characteristics identified in one week will also be identified in a subsequent week. The 1984 National Election Study provides us with a chance to look for crystallization over the course of the nominating season.

The NES asked respondents about twelve traits for each candidate. These traits include competence, empathy, integrity, and leadership. Competence is assessed by ratings on the adjectives "hardworking," "intelligent," and "knowledgeable." Empathy is covered by "compassionate," "kind," and "really cares." Integrity is represented by "decent," "moral," and "good example." Leadership is assessed by "commands respect," "inspiring," and "strong leader." Respondents were asked whether the adjective "fits your impression" of the candidate "a great deal," "somewhat," "a little," or "not at all."

To measure distinctness, we have taken the means of the twelve traits for the twenty-five weeks from January 11 to June 19, and we have examined how the standard deviation of the twelve trait averages changed from week to week. In this context the standard deviation serves as a measure of how much the means for the same candidate vary across the different traits. For well-known candidates with distinct images we expected that the standard deviation of the twelve traits would be relatively large—on average our respondents would give quite different answers to questions about different traits. For less well-known candidates we expected the standard deviations to be small because, on average, most people would not give very different answers to questions about different traits. Finally, as time went on and more was learned about the candidate, we expected that the standard deviation would become larger.

To measure stability, we have analyzed how the correlation between one week's averages and the next week's have changed over time. For well-known candidates with stable images we expected that one week's traits would be highly correlated with those of the next week while for less well-known candidates the correlations would be lower as their images changed from week to week. And, as more was learned about a candidate, we expected that the weekly correlation would tend towards unity (more precisely, to .985 which is the theoretical maximum as a result of the noisiness of the small samples available for each week).

Figure 4.8 plots the correlations over time. Not surprisingly, these correlations vary a great deal from week to week. Part of this variation is undoubtedly due to the very small samples from which the correlations were calculated, but part of it may also reflect the action of various campaign events which change the images of the candidates. To summarize the overall trends in these correlations, we have fitted some straight lines to them for each candidate. The slopes and intercepts of these lines are reported in Table 4.3. The slope indicates how much the measure of stability (i.e., the correlation) for the candidate changes from week to week. Note that the slope for the correlations is essentially zero for Ronald Reagan, indicating no change over time, slightly positive for Walter Mondale, and significantly positive for Jackson, Hart, and Glenn, indicating substantial change over time. The intercept in each of these equations is the best estimate of the true correlation between the traits on January 11th and January 18th. Hence, they can be interpreted as the stability of each candidate's image at the beginning of the primary season. The intercepts reveal the same picture as the slopes: Mondale and Reagan presented very stable images from the beginning (an average correlation of about .92). Hart, Jackson and Glenn started out with relatively low correlations (between .80 for Hart and .84 for Glenn) and slowly increased the stability of their images to the level of Mondale and Reagan.

A figure for the standard deviations reveals a similar pattern, and the corresponding straight lines are also reported in Table 4.3. Hart and Glenn seem to form one group with high slopes (.0055 and .0045) and small intercepts (.126 and .223), Mondale and Jackson seem to form another with moderate slopes (.0024 and .0016) and moderate intercepts (.285 and .255) and Reagan is in a separate class with a slope that is essentially zero and a larger intercept (.325). As expected, the images of Reagan and Mondale were distinct to begin with and did not change very much. The images of Hart and Glenn were indistinct at first, and they became much more differentiated over the course of the primary season while the images of Reagan and Mondale were distinct to begin with and did not change very much. The data for Jackson tell an interesting story. His image was fairly distinct from the beginning, undoubtedly as a consequence of the saturation coverage he received for his trip to Syria in the first few weeks of January just before the rolling cross-section began, but his image was not very stable. This instability mirrors the ups and downs of the UPI stories on Jackson's

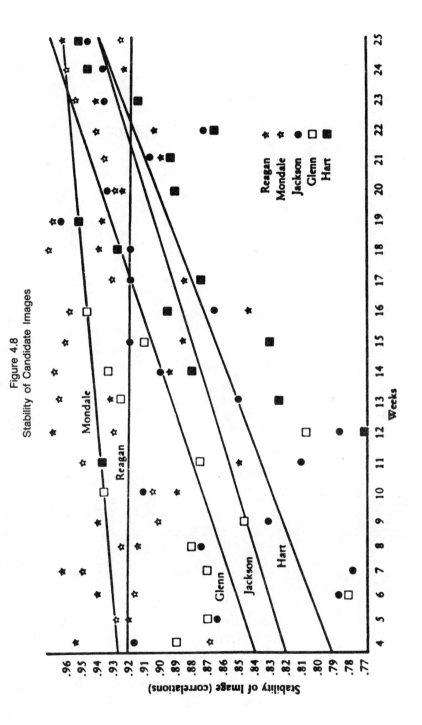

Figure 4.8
Stability of Candidate Images

TABLE 4.3   Trends in Distinctness and Stability

Candidate	Slope	Intercept	R Squared
	Distinctness (Standard Deviations)		
Reagan	.0003 (.0012)	.325 (.090)	.003
Mondale	.0024 (.0014)	.285 (.101)	.132
Jackson	.0016 (.0011)	.255 (.081)	.092
Glenn	.0045 (.0014)	.223 (.039)	.447
Hart	.0055 (.0016)	.126 (.032)	.476
	Stability (Correlations)		
Reagan	-.0001 (.0011)	.919 (.074)	.000
Mondale	.0016 (.0008)	.922 (.056)	.150
Jackson	.0050 (.0015)	.824 (.010)	.365
Glenn	.0065 (.0033)	.841 (.075)	.263
Hart	.0063 (.0028)	.794 (.049)	.286

personal qualities and his leadership ability as he went from media hero after his trip to Syria to media goat in his comments about "Hymie-town."

People do learn about candidates during the primaries. But they probably learn too late about some candidates such as Glenn and McGovern who dropped out by the tenth week of our surveys (in the first month of the primary season). Moreover, it seems as if the images of political newcomers become more distinct and stable over time. If one believes that distinctness and stability are good because they insure that voters have a refined image of the candidates, then the primary process can be commended because it produces distinct and stable images. But it takes time to do this, and the preceding analysis can be used to determine how long it would take any of our candidates to reach a predetermined level of distinctness and stability.

Consider, for example, Gary Hart. Let us assume that the distinctness and stability of Walter Mondale's image during the first week of our survey (January 11–18) is a reasonable amount of image crystallization. According to Table 4.3, the distinctness of Mondale's image, using the standard deviation of the traits as a measure of distinctness, was .285 in early January, and the stability of Mondale's image at this same time, using the correlation of the traits as a measure, was .922. Some simple calculations based upon the results for Hart in Table 4.3 indicate that it would took him thirty weeks to reach this level of distinctness (starting at .126 and proceeding at the rate of .0055 per week) and twenty weeks to reach this level of stability (starting at .794 and proceeding at the rate of .0063 per week). Since the primary season was completed by the twenty-first week of our survey, it appears as if the voters chose between Hart and Mondale before Hart had an image that was as distinct and stable as Walter Mondale's during the middle of January.

Viability and Media Coverage. It is disturbing to learn that it takes so long for our national sample to learn about the traits of candidates, but it would be much less disturbing, possibly even pleasing, to learn that citizens take a long time to learn about the viabilities of the candidates. Unfortunately, we shall show that voters learn very quickly about who's ahead and who's behind in the horse-race called by the media.

It is an easy matter to show that voters are attentive to the horse-race. Figure 4.9 plots a smoothed version (using a three period simple moving average) of the daily average viability ratings for Glenn, Hart, Jackson, and Mondale from February 1st until March 31st. (The question about Hart was not asked until after New Hampshire.) Viabilities are measured by the NES 100 point viability scales where "100" indicates that the candidate will certainly win and "0" indicates that the candidate will certainly lose. These averages tend to jump around because of the very small samples involved (typically five to fifteen), but when plotted together, they suggest that the respondents to the NES had some very concrete notions of the horse-race. Glenn started off fairly high, but he quickly nose-dived with his biggest decline right after his poor showing in New Hampshire. Jackson remained low throughout the entire period. Finally, although we are lacking the early data on Hart, it is not surprising that the viabilities for Mondale and Hart in the NES surveys are strongly negatively correlated with one another. For the entire period from just

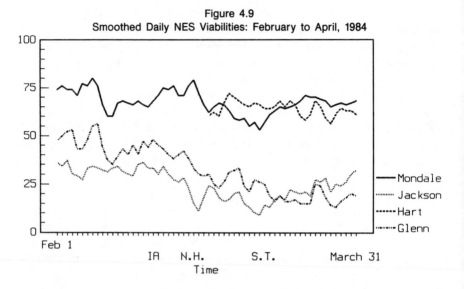

Figure 4.9
Smoothed Daily NES Viabilities: February to April, 1984

after New Hampshire to the end of July, Hart and Mondale's viabilities are correlated at −.44.

We also found this negative correlation in the UPI data. This suggests that people might be getting their notions of the horse-race from the media. As a first-step towards demonstrating this relationship, we have developed a Bayesian learning model to explain changes in beliefs about viabilities. According to Bayesian models of knowledge and information, an individual's opinion about a topic such as candidate viability is not just a number like "80 percent chance of winning." Rather, it is a probability distribution over all the possible chances of winning. If the person knows very little about a candidate's chance of winning, then this distribution is very flat with a large variance—the person assigns approximately equal probability to all possible answers. On the other hand, if the person knows a great deal about the candidate's chance of winning, then the distribution will be very pointed with a very small variance—the person assigns very high probabilities to a narrow range of answers and very low probabilities to all the rest. At any given moment, an individual has some probability distribution which is called the person's "prior beliefs." If some information about viability, say a media report, is heard or read, then Bayesian decision theory suggests that the person will "update" his or her prior beliefs according to a rule called Bayes' Law. This updating amounts to coming up with a new probability distribution which describes the person's "posterior beliefs." We have used this rule to develop an equation which relates the UPI media reports to the NES measures of viability.

The equation is derived from a model which assumes normally distributed prior beliefs and normally distributed information with each line of coverage considered a separate piece of information. With these assumptions, we can show how the mean of the posterior distribution of beliefs is related to prior beliefs and to the UPI coverage. The mean of the posterior distribution is called V^*_{ijt}—person i's best guess about candidate j's viability at time t. This is equal to the weighted average of the person's initial V_{j0} assessment of candidate j's viability at time zero (the mean of the person's prior distribution) and the media viability V_{jt} based upon the average of all media reports from time one to the current period.[5] The weights in the weighted average consist of the strength of one's prior beliefs S_j and the number of reports received about the candidate's viability N_{jt}. The quantities V_{j0}, V_{jt}, S_j and N_{jt} do not have the subscript i because we assume, for simplicity, that they are constant across individuals:

$$V^*_{ijt} = \frac{S_j V_{j0} + N_{jt} V_{jt}}{S_j + N_{jt}} \qquad (1)$$

This formula is best understood by considering some polar cases. Suppose that no messages have been received so that N_{jt} is zero, then V^*_{ijt} equals one's prior beliefs for the candidate's viability. This seems sensible; if no outside information is available, then one must be guided by prior beliefs. On the other hand, if the number of messages received is infinite (or very large compared to the strength S_j of the person's prior beliefs), then V^*_{ijt} equals the average viability, V_{jt}, based upon media reports. This is also sensible; if there is a great deal of outside information then prior beliefs should be ignored. In the in-between cases, equation (1) provides an intuitively sensible rule for combining, by a weighted average, the mean value of prior beliefs and the mean value of new information provided by the media.

By assuming that this is a reasonable model of how people process information, this equation can be used to explore the relationship between the UPI reports and the NES viability measures. Person i's viability estimate V^*_{ijt} for candidate j at time t can be measured by the one-hundred point NES viability scale. We can measure V_{jt} by taking the average of the UPI evaluations of viability coverage from the initial period to the current period. We can measure the number of reports received about the candidate's viability N_{jt} by the number of lines of viability coverage on the candidate from time zero to time t. There is a complication, however. The NES and UPI measures of viability involve scales with different zero points (zero for the NES versus minus two for the UPI) and different units (one hundred points versus five points),

TABLE 4.4   Bayesian Learning of Viability, 1984 (Standard Errors)

	s_j	v_{jo}	$s_j * v_{jo}$	α	β	r^2	S.E.
Glenn	100	55.5 (310)	5,546 (2.45)	10.99 (5.32)	18.02	.2366	22.83
Hart	500	65.8 (1424)	32,894 (3.67)	-21.88 (3.47)	69.10	.1857	23.41
Jackson	10	169.8 (247)	1,698 (1.34)	17.91 (7.41)	21.72	.0187	24.62
Mondale	1500	58.3 (2801)	87,411 (12.34)	8.18 (22.20)	51.79	.0499	23.82

and they must differ by at least a linear transformation. Hence, we introduce the parameters α and β to adjust for these differences:

$$V_{ijt}^* = \frac{S_j V_{j0} + \alpha N_{jt} + \beta N_{jt} V_{jt}}{S_j + N_{jt}} \quad (2)$$

Equation (2) presents a complicated non-linear estimation problem because of the unknown parameter S_j in the denominator. Our solution to this problem has been to estimate different versions of (2) with various values of S_j and to choose that case with the smallest sum of squared residuals. This has the disadvantage of not providing any information on the standard error in our estimate of S_j, but it does yield consistent estimates of all the parameters in the model.[6]

Table 4.4 presents estimates of S_j, V_{j0}, α, and β for each candidate. Because NES viability estimates were not obtained for Hart until after New Hampshire, the initial period for Hart was just after he had scored a major victory in late February in New Hampshire. The Glenn and Mondale equations were estimated starting in the middle of January before any caucuses or primaries. The best fits (R^2 values) are obtained for Glenn and Hart and the worst for Jesse Jackson. The fit for Mondale is in between. This seems very reasonable because John Glenn and Gary Hart's viabilities exhibited the most variability and Jesse Jackson's exhibited the least. Moreover, we know from the UPI data that there was a great deal of viability coverage for Glenn, Hart, and Mondale, and very little for Jesse Jackson (see Figures 4.5 and 4.7). Because the Jackson equation does so poorly, we will ignore it in the following discussion.

The estimates of the strength S_j of prior beliefs suggest that people had the strongest priors about Walter Mondale and the weakest priors about John Glenn. This is quite reasonable because people knew a great deal about Walter Mondale in mid-January before the primary season began. They knew much less about John Glenn at this time. By early March when the Hart data was first collected, the events of the previous weeks, the Iowa caucuses and the New Hampshire primary, had provided voters with the first real data about the candidates' chances, although these events had also created a good deal of uncertainty about who would win the nomination.

The initial estimates of viability V_{j0} also reflect the conditions at the time. Mondale was seen as having a better chance than Glenn in mid-January—although the difference between these two estimates is less than we might have expected. The value for Hart reflects his impressive showing in New Hampshire.

Probably the most important results are the statistical and substantive significance of α and β. These parameters are the heart of the Bayesian model, and their significance indicates that people do "learn" from media reports. In the best of all worlds, we would expect that all values of α and all values of β would be the same across the four candidates. We are not so lucky, but they are all statistically significant and within a range that seems reasonable given the NES and UPI measures of viability. If the UPI measure could be mapped directly into the NES measure, then we would expect that α would be around 50 and β would be around 25. (That is, zero on the NES scale would correspond to minus two on the UPI scale and one hundred on the NES scale would correspond to plus two on the UPI scale.) However, while evaluations on the NES scale get near zero for Glenn and Jackson, they hardly ever get near minus two on the UPI scale. Indeed, evaluations on the UPI scale range between $-.33$ and 1.33, and those on the NES scale range between zero and one hundred. Hence, we probably should expect a value of about twenty for α and about sixty for β. The estimates reported in Table 4.4 jump around more than this, but they are in this range.

These results are preliminary, and they certainly do not prove that media coverage leads to viability assessments. They do suggest, however, that the two are strongly related to one another. In the future, we intend to investigate this relationship in more detail with a more sophisticated equation and better estimation methods. For example, we intend to undertake exogeneity tests to determine the direction of causality and to pin-down the leads and lags in the relationship between media coverage and public perceptions of the candidates. Until we have finished those analyses, the results in Table 4.4 provide some of the best evidence that viability assessments by the media are converted into viability estimates by the citizenry.

Conclusions

People do learn about candidates from the media. However, their learning about the substantive characteristics of the candidates takes a long time, while their learning about viability occurs quickly. This is not surprising given the imperatives of the media's search for a good story, but it is distressing for two reasons. First, viability information is the result of media decision rules whose logic is different from the putative logic of the current nominating process. The media are interested in a good story. The nominating process seeks a good candidate. Iowa usually produces a good story, but the "good story" in Iowa may not be a "good candidate." The requirements for a good story often lead to an exaggeration of a candidate's performance and a simplification of reality. The desire for a good candidate should lead to a relatively modest appraisal of the meaning of Gary Hart's winning several thousand more votes in Iowa than George McGovern. As we have seen, the media's reaction was anything but modest.

In another paper (Brady, 1987), I have developed a mathematical model of the nominating process which shows how a nominating process with harsh media judgments performs like a "lottery whose odds are fixed by the news media." In this paper, I have argued that the media do make harsh judgments about candidates. These judgments, then, lead to a process in which candidates may be eliminated from the race or catapulted to fame based upon the most meager evidence of their merits or demerits.

The second problem with viability information is that voters often use it as a major basis for their voting decision because it is more readily available than other forms of information about the candidates. There is, of course, some substantive information in viabilities, but this content is actually very, very small (Brady and Hagen, 1986). It is so small, in fact, that a voter relying upon it is not doing much better than choosing randomly.

In sum, Iowa is news, but democracy may not be served by that fact.

Epilogue

The body of this paper was written before the 1988 Iowa caucuses and the unfolding of the 1988 campaign. Unlike many other years, the winners in Iowa went nowhere in 1988. Bob Dole won with 37.3 percent of the preference vote, Pat Robertson obtained 24.6 percent, and George Bush received only 18.6 percent, but Bush went on to win handily in New Hampshire with 37.8 percent of the vote to Dole's 28.4 percent and to win the nomination. On the Democratic side, Richard Gephardt won Iowa with 31.3 percent of the delegates, Paul Simon was a close second with 26.7 percent, and Michael Dukakis took third place with only 22.1 percent of the vote, but Dukakis also went on to a strong win in New Hampshire (35.8 percent to Gephardt's 19.8 percent) and the eventual nomination.[7] If Iowa is so important, then, why these results? Why did Richard Gephardt's campaign and Bob Dole's campaign fall apart so quickly? Without the kind of data reported above, I cannot provide a detailed answer to these questions. This epilogue, then, must be necessarily speculative.

A clear-cut story can be told about the Democratic campaign. Based upon my observations of the news the night of the Iowa caucuses (Brady, 1988), I think it is fair to say that the Democratic story was deemphasized relative to the Republican story. All three networks led with Bush's "poor" third place finish, Dole's victory, and Robertson's surprising showing. Despite the fact that he won 31.3 percent of the delegates— just about double the showing of Hart in 1984, Gephardt was given surprisingly little coverage. This may be because Gephardt was from a neighboring state (Missouri) or because he spent more time in Iowa than any other candidate. However, Hart's home state, Colorado, is also close to Iowa, and Hart spent an enormous amount of time in Iowa in 1984. Yet Hart's poorer second-place showing received a great deal of coverage in 1984. Maybe the media were trying not to repeat their mistakes of 1988, but it seems more likely that the Republican story simply drove out coverage of the Democratic story. The big difference between 1984 and 1988, then, was two competitive nominations instead of only one, and in these circumstances, the media tried to simplify matters by focussing on only one race. The Dole, Robertson, Bush result was perfect for their needs: Bush as champion, Dole as challenger, and Robertson as human interest.

This may explain Gephardt's failure to benefit from momentum in 1988, but only at the cost of making the Republican results seem more enigmatic. If the media really focussed on the Republican race, then why didn't Dole (not to mention Robertson) do much better in New Hampshire? This is harder to explain. One answer is that Dole in 1988 was much better known than Hart in 1984, Carter in 1976, or McGovern in 1972. There are many reasons to believe that candidates will profit less from momentum when they are well-known (Bartels, 1988; Brady, 1984a, 1984b, 1987; Brady and Ansolabehere, forthcoming). Another answer may interact with this. George Bush undoubtedly has a keen and painful memory of losing the "big 'mo'" to Ronald Reagan after Iowa in 1980, and in 1988, he went all out just before the New Hampshire primary by using hard-hitting negative advertising to attack Bob Dole. This effort may have played upon what the voters thought they knew about Dole to diminish the impact of Iowa. Indeed, some of the polls reported around the time of the New Hampshire primary indicated that Dole did receive a "jolt" from his success in Iowa, but this momentum evaporated over the weekend before the New Hampshire primary.

Whether or not these explanations will hold-up when data become available for analysis, the results of Iowa in 1988 serve as a warning to those who would make too much of media power. This is salutary. I, for one, do not believe that the media are all powerful. Rather, I believe that media effects are contingent, and they are most important when voters (and members of the media) know very little about a candidate and when events move very swiftly. These conditions held most strongly in Iowa in 1976 with Jimmy Carter and in 1984 with Gary Hart. In these cases, media judgments can and did have a great impact on the outcome of the nomination process.

Notes

This paper draws upon joint work with Michael Hagen. Larry Bartels has been a constant source of support and encouragement. Patti Conley provided outstanding research assistance in a frenetic atmosphere. Chris Achen inspired the epilogue. Many others, too numerous to name, helped me in one way or another.

1. There were no Republican straw votes in Iowa in 1972 and 1984 when strong incumbents (Nixon and Reagan) were running for renomination.

2. The stories were obtained from an online database called "Dialog." A computer search algorithm was used which chose any story containing one of the last names of the eight major Democratic candidates. After coding it became apparent to us that some days around the California primary appeared to have less coverage than we expected. As a check on our results, we obtained a completely new and independently collected set of 1984 stories from the "Nexis" database. We found substantial overlap between these two sets of data, but, as we suspected, the Dialog database appears to be deficient around the time of the California primary. We are now in the process of fixing up this problem by coding the Nexis data as a supplement to the Dialog data. In the interim, for the following analyses we have adjusted the Dialog codings by multiplying them by the inverse of the fraction of Nexis stories which appear in the Dialog database. For almost all weeks, these fractions are about .85, but they dip to as low as .11 for the week of the California primary.

3. The smoothing was done by taking the simple average of seven days of coverage centered on the current observation. We took the average of three days before the observation, the observation itself, and three days after the observation. We excluded four states, Idaho, North Dakota, Vermont, and Wisconsin from our analyses of either primaries or caucuses because they select delegates through caucuses *and* have "non-binding" primaries as well.

4. A similar set of runs using the "location" variable lead to the same conclusions. The only major difference is that the effects for Iowa and New Hampshire are, if anything, much more impressive.

5. Note that when $t = 0$, V_{jt} is simply the mean of the person's prior beliefs. This makes sense because we do not have any measures of media reports until time one.

6. The actual model that was estimated includes an additional factor that discounts S_j over time. This was done because we assumed that people would heavily discount older information—especially prior beliefs. Thus, in the denominator of (2), S_j was multiplied by $.995^{t-1}$. This implies a daily discount of .005 or one half percent per day. This adjustment improves the fit of the model, but it is somewhat ad hoc. We are now in the process of estimating a theoretically more pleasing model which incorporates discounting of the media reports as well as prior beliefs.

7. These results are from *Congressional Quarterly Weekly Report*, July 9, 1988.

References

Bartels, Larry. 1988. *Presidential Primaries and the Dynamics of Public Choice.* Princeton: Princeton University Press.

Brady, Henry E. 1984a. Chances, Utilities, and Voting in Presidential Primaries. Paper presented at a conference sponsored by the California Institute of Technology.

_____. 1984b. Computer Assisted Survey Methods andPresidential Primaries. *Election Politics.*

_____. 1987. Knowledge, Strategy, and Momentum inPresidential Primaries. Working Paper, Harvard University.

_____. 1988. Strategy on the Campaign Trail. *PS: Political Science and Politics,* 21:269–273.

_____, and Stephen Ansolabehere. Forthcoming. The Nature of Utility Functions in Mass Publics. *American Political Science Review.*

_____, and Michael Hagen. 1986. The 'Horse-Race' or the Issues: What's the Primary Message? Paper presented at the annual meetings of the American Political Science Association, Washington, D.C.

_____, and Richard Johnston. 1987. What's the Primary Message: Horse Race or Issue Journalism. In Gary R. Orren and Nelson W. Polsby, eds., *Media and Momentum.* Chatham, NJ: Chatham House.

5

After Iowa: Momentum in Presidential Primaries

Larry M. Bartels

Once every four years on a winter evening the good people of Iowa gather in their schoolhouses and living rooms and have their say. But what happens then? The next morning, if recent history is any guide, America has a new political star.

This pattern has been repeated, with minor variations, in three recent primary seasons. Jimmy Carter in 1976, George Bush in 1980, and Gary Hart in 1984 each managed to parlay a "better than expected" showing in Iowa into media attention, recognition, and public support sufficient to make a serious run at his party's nomination. Carter made it all the way to the White House, and Bush and Hart did not stop trying.

I do not want to claim any special expertise in making sense of what happens in those schoolhouses and living rooms on caucus night. I leave that to my colleagues—or, if academics dare not tread, to the experts of the press corps. My own aim is to suggest how and why whatever happens on that evening shapes, for better or worse, what happens in the other forty-nine fiftieths of the presidential nominating process.

My analysis is in five parts. First, I describe the phenomenon of "momentum" in recent presidential nominating politics, with particular emphasis on the role of the Iowa caucuses in generating momentum. In the next two sections I describe the underpinnings of momentum in the psychology of prospective primary voters, focusing first on the impact of information and second on the impact of expectations about the outcome of the race. I then consider how momentum may be blunted, both by its own internal dynamics and by broader political considerations. Finally, I address some of the significant issues of institutional design flowing from the role of momentum in presidential primaries.

"Big Mo"

By now it is a political truism that small events in Iowa can have big effects on the rest of the presidential campaign. But it was not always thus. In 1974, Hamilton Jordan wrote a long memorandum outlining the political strategy for Jimmy Carter's incipient presidential campaign. Jordan's plan recognized many of the strategic possibilities inherent in the new media-oriented, primary-dominated nominating process. "The press shows an exaggerated interest in the early primaries," he wrote (Witcover 1977, pp. 143–146). "Good or poor showings can have a profound and irrevocable impact on succeeding primaries and a candidate's abilities to raise funds and recruit workers." He recommended that Carter concentrate his campaign in two of the first primary states, New Hampshire and Florida, hoping to win one or the other outright while knocking off George Wallace in the South. The initial delegate selections in non-primary states, Jordan wrote, "will generate some news stories and will be important, but in the long run they will take a back seat to the coverage of the primaries."

Fortunately for Carter, Jordan's plan was flexible on the last point. With the press—and especially R. W. Apple of the *New York Times*—devoting unprecedented attention to the intricacies of Iowa's first-in-the-nation caucuses, Carter's strategy was amended to take advantage of what the candidate himself called "a good chance to build that up with a major media event" (Schram, 1977, p. 8). The result, as Schram put it later (1977, p. 22):

> Just 50,000 Iowans had gone to the [Democratic] caucuses. Fewer than 14,000 of them voted for Jimmy Carter. In Oyster Bay, Long Island, that would not be enough votes to elect him to the Town Council. But in Iowa, it was more than any other candidate got. In the morning, he appeared on NBC's "Today" show, the CBS "Morning News," and ABC's "AM America." Jimmy Carter had popped out of the pack.

By 1980 it was widely recognized that Iowa would be a crucial launching pad for any relatively unknown candidate hoping to emerge as Carter had in 1976. As it turned out, George Bush went Carter one better in Iowa, not only winning but upsetting his party's well-established front runner for the nomination, Ronald Reagan. Bush's margin of victory amounted to less than 10,000 votes out of 150,000 cast in a state where Reagan did almost no campaigning. But the impact of that victory on the complexion of the race was revolutionary. The cover story in *Newsweek* announced: "Bush Breaks Out of the Pack." Polls of the Republican rank and file suddenly had Bush and Reagan dead even. And Washington insiders at a National Press Club luncheon picked Bush over Reagan as the likely nominee by a margin of six to one (Greenfield, 1982, p. 12).

Since Bush's campaign was directly modelled on Carter's four years earlier, success in Iowa's "functional equivalent of a primary"[1] was a crucial selling point for the primaries to come—a fact which Bush himself took no pains to conceal. Looking forward to the New Hampshire primary, Bush told Bob Schieffer on the CBS "Morning" show (quoted by Greenfield, 1982, pp. 39–40) that "what we'll have, you see, is momentum. We will have forward 'Big Mo' on our side, as they say in athletics."

" 'Big Mo'?" Schieffer asked.

"Yeah," Bush replied, " 'Mo,' momentum."

Having invented "forward 'Big Mo' " after Iowa, Bush went on to discover backward "Big Mo" a few weeks later in New Hampshire. He quickly dropped the whole idea, but the press transferred it intact to other candidates, both in 1980 and in more recent campaigns.

In any objective sense, Gary Hart in 1984 was considerably less successful in Iowa than either Jimmy Carter in 1976 or George Bush in 1980. Hart garnered about 15 percent of the Democratic caucus vote, well behind Walter Mondale with 45 percent. But John Glenn's campaign was in the process of disintegrating, and Hart's 15 percent made him the most interesting alternative to Mondale. Bruce Morton on CBS said of Hart, "when you lose three-to-one, you've lost" (Adams, 1985, p. 12). Nevertheless, the headline in the next morning's *New York Times* declared "The Campaign Reshaped." *Newsweek* featured "Hart's Charge," with the blue-eyed candidate smiling from the cover. Despite Mondale's convincing victory, Hart got more—and more favorable—media coverage than Mondale in the subsequent week, leading up to the crucial first primary in New Hampshire. Indeed, Hart got more coverage than Mondale for the rest of the primary season, after having received only one third as much before Iowa (Brady and Johnston, 1987, pp. 145, 147). As Robinson and Sheehan (1983, p. 80) put it, "access belongs to those who beat the political odds."

Hart parlayed his media access into a big victory in New Hampshire. He beat Mondale by almost ten percentage points, after having trailed by a three-to-one margin only eight days earlier (Moore, 1985, p. 5). He won again—with seventy percent of the primary vote—the following week in Vermont. There was talk that Mondale might quit the race; but instead he redoubled his efforts in the Super Tuesday primaries in Georgia and Alabama and managed to stave off Hart's last chance for an early knockout. It wasn't pretty, but Mondale had survived to continue the fight in more congenial states, including Illinois, New York, and

Pennsylvania in the subsequent month. In the end, Hart garnered a near-plurality of the total primary vote and won fifteen primaries to Mondale's ten. It was a striking performance, but not enough to win the nomination.[2]

The Impact of Information

One of the most significant facts about presidential nominating campaigns—a fact distinguishing them sharply from general election campaigns—is that the competing candidates vary widely in the extent to which they begin the campaign as familiar public figures. This fact is illustrated in Table 5.1, which shows the percentage of the public claiming to "know something about" each of the candidates in early stages of recent nominating campaigns. At one extreme, prospective candidates like Gerald Ford, Edward Kennedy, and Jesse Jackson have entered the primary arena already known to virtually the entire population. At the opposite extreme, candidates like Lloyd Bentsen, Philip Crane, and Bruce Babbitt have begun with very low levels of public recognition.

For the less fortunate candidates, like Bentsen and Crane, running for president is nothing more and nothing less than a constant (and ultimately unsuccessful) struggle to put themselves before the public. But there is one way to break out of the vicious circle of non-recognition and non-support: by doing "better than expected" in an early primary or caucus. The news media lavish so much coverage on Iowa and New Hampshire—and especially on candidates who do unexpectedly well in those states—that a relative unknown can be vaulted into public prominence in a matter of days.

This fact is documented in Figure 5.1, which shows weekly levels of public familiarity for three candidates—Walter Mondale, Gary Hart, and Reubin Askew—for the 23 weeks of the 1984 primary season, from mid-January (Week 1) to mid-June (Week 23).[3] Mondale is typical of candidates who begin the primary season as familiar public figures; the proportion of each week's survey sample who knew something about him ranged, for the most part, between 90 and 100 percent.[4] Askew is typical of candidates who start out relatively unknown and never do succeed in attracting the notice of the public; he ended the primary season about where he began it, known to roughly half of the survey respondents. Hart is the most interesting case, the one candidate in 1984 who succeeded in emerging from the pack into the forefront of public consciousness.

The magnitude of Hart's emergence is dramatic. In January he, like Askew, was familiar to a little more than 40 percent of the public; by the end of the primary season his level of familiarity was just below

TABLE 5.1   Familiarity with Primary Candidates, 1976-1988

Percentage of Party Identifiers Who Say They "Know Something About" Candidate at Beginning of Primary Season

1988	Hart	---	Bush	89
	Jackson	81	Robertson	61
	Dukakis	29	Haig	57
	Gore	23	Dole	56
	Simon	22	Kemp	30
	Gephardt	19	Du Pont	14
	Babbitt	16		
1984	Glenn	94.1		
	Mondale	93.6		
	Jackson	93.6		
	McGovern	93.1		
	Cranston	63.8		
	Hart	46.3		
	Askew	41.5		
	Hollings	36.7		
1980	Carter	98.4	Reagan	92.0
	Kennedy	94.8	Connally	72.9
	Brown	63.9	Baker	53.4
			Bush	46.6
			Dole	41.9
			Crane	7.7
			Anderson	----
1976	Wallace	73.8	Ford	90.8
	Shriver	44.3	Reagan	81.6
	Jackson	29.1		
	Udall	23.4		
	Bayh	22.2		
	Carter	21.5		
	Church	21.1		
	Harris	12.9		
	Bentsen	7.3		

Sources: **1988**   October 1987 Gallup Poll; 726 Democrats and 678 Republicans.

1984   January-February (pre-Iowa) National Election Study survey; 188 Democrats (percentage willing to rate candidates on "feeling" thermometer).

1980   January-February (post-Iowa, pre-New Hampshire) National Election Study survey; 504 Democrats and 339 Republicans.

1976   February (post-Iowa, pre-New Hampshire) Patterson survey in Los Angeles and Erie Pennsylvania; 573 Democrats and 293 Republicans.

Figure 5.1
Familiarity with Mondale, Hart, and Askew: 1984

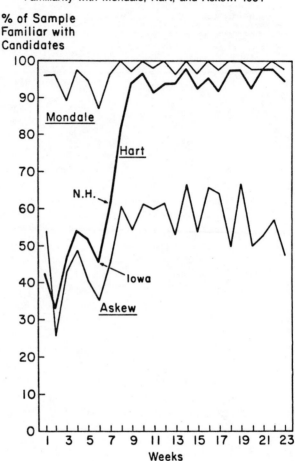

Mondale's, at about 95 percent. But what is even more striking is the suddenness of the emergence evident in Figure 5.1. Almost all of the manifest public learning about Hart, at least at this relatively superficial level, occurred in the three-week window beginning with his second-place finish in Iowa, continuing with his dramatic primary victories in New Hampshire and Vermont, and ending with the Hart-Mondale standoff on Super Tuesday. The rate at which prospective voters came to know something about Hart during this period provides a remarkable example of the potential impact of early electoral success (and consequent media attention) on the political consciousness of the public. For three weeks, if we can extrapolate from these figures, Hart was becoming known to between 25 and 30 million people each week. As the candidate himself put it (WGBH, 1984), "You can get awful famous in this country in seven days."

Prospective voters will almost never support a candidate they don't know at least something about. Thus, part of the political significance of Hart's sudden fame stems from the simple fact that he was becoming a live alternative for millions of people who hadn't previously considered him. But even beyond the threshold level of familiarity necessary to become a live alternative, candidates' support levels tend to increase, other things being equal, as the public learns more about them. Like people making many other sorts of choices, prospective voters tend to prefer a relatively certain prospect to a more uncertain one. In the language of decision theorists, they tend to be "risk averse."

Learning about Hart in this more general sense occurred not only during his three-week breakout between Iowa and Super Tuesday, but also—though more gradually—throughout the remainder of the primary season. By the same token, prospective voters learned more about Mondale as the campaign went on, even though he had already crossed the threshold of superficial familiarity for more than nine out of then of them before it began. This learning is evident in Figure 5.2, which shows estimated average levels of public information about Hart and Mondale for each week of the 1984 campaign.[5]

The political impact of information on choices between Hart and Mondale—due both to the threshold effect of minimal familiarity and to the more general effect of risk aversion—is shown in Figure 5.3. For each of three hypothetical evaluations ("feeling thermometer" ratings), the figure shows how the probability of supporting a candidate varied with prospective voters' information about that candidate (measured on the same scale shown in Figure 5.2). For low levels of information— for example, the average level for Hart at the beginning of the 1984 campaign, labelled "Early" in the figure—even those respondents who evaluated a candidate fairly favorably were very unlikely to support him. This portion of the figure is consistent with the notion that some minimal level of familiarity is virtually a necessary condition for supporting any candidate.

The remainder of Figure 5.3 shows that support increased dramatically with increasing information, first among those respondents most favorably inclined toward a candidate on other grounds, but eventually among those less favorably inclined as well. The total gains in support for Hart attributable directly to his emergence into the public consciousness between mid-January ("Early") and mid-June ("Late") ranged from more than sixty percentage points among respondents who viewed him very

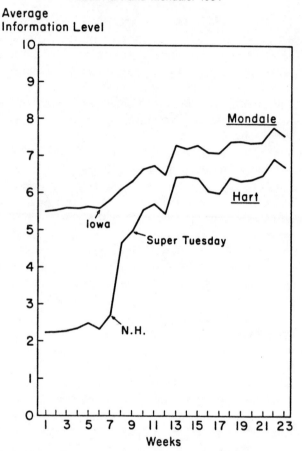

Figure 5.2
Average Levels of Information
About Hart and Mondale: 1984

favorably to about fifteen percentage points even among those who were moderately unfavorable toward him on substantive grounds.

These results make it clear why, from the candidates' point of view, being well known is a very considerable political resource—and why the amount of information prospective voters acquired about Gary Hart in the weeks after the Iowa caucuses was a very significant factor in the 1984 campaign. Candidates who are well known to the public at least have a chance to attract widespread political support. Candidates who remain unknown do not. Candidates like Hart, who go from being unknown to being well known in a matter of days or weeks, go from certain defeat to potential victory.

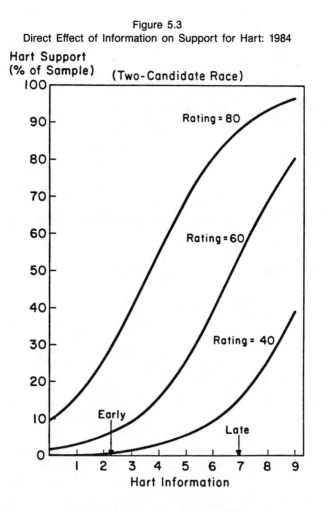

Figure 5.3
Direct Effect of Information on Support for Hart: 1984

Hart Support
(% of Sample)   (Two-Candidate Race)

The Impact of Expectations

A strong showing in Iowa can not only vault a formerly unknown candidate into public prominence; it can also recast public perceptions of the candidate's chances of winning the nomination. I have already noted the revolutionary effect of Bush's 1980 Iowa upset on the expectations of an elite audience about his chances of winning the nomination. But the intensive focus of the news media throughout the primary season on the campaign "horse race"—who is winning, who is gaining ground, who is doing better than expected—provides even ordinarily attentive members of the general public with abundant raw material for handicapping the candidates' chances (Patterson, 1980; Robinson and Sheehan,

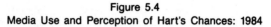

Figure 5.4
Media Use and Perception of Hart's Chances: 1984

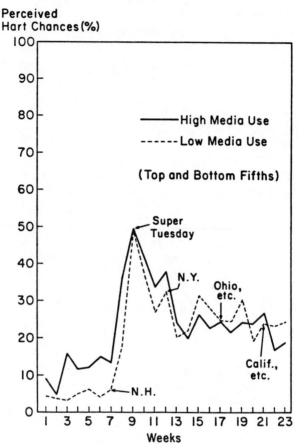

1983; Brady and Johnston, 1987). Indeed, Robinson and Clancey (1985, p. 61) concluded from their more general study of the media and political information that "people knew more about winners and losers in primaries than they knew about anything else."

The responsiveness of expectations to campaign events is evident in Figure 5.4, which shows how perceptions of Gary Hart's chances varied from week to week during the 1984 primary season.[6] The figure shows separate time trends for two distinct groups of respondents, the fifth of the sample most exposed and attentive to the news media and the fifth of the sample least exposed and attentive to the news media. Hart's perceived chances surged among both groups, albeit somewhat more quickly among heavy media users, after his big primary victory in New

Hampshire. His high water mark came just before Super Tuesday, when both groups gave him an even chance to win the nomination. But Mondale managed to hold Hart to what the press interpreted as a draw in the Super Tuesday primaries, and during the subsequent month Hart's perceived chances of winning the nomination declined precipitously while Mondale's increased. During the last two months of the campaign, with Mondale well in the lead in the delegate race, public perceptions of Hart's chances remained relatively stable at between twenty and thirty percent, more or less regardless of media use.

The public's changing perceptions of the candidates' chances would be of little more than incidental interest if people kept horse race perceptions and substantive political considerations in separate, watertight mental compartments. But there are a variety of reasons to believe that prospective voters' substantive judgments and choices do depend in part on their expectations about the candidates' chances of winning the nomination.[7] For one thing, prospective voters may choose a candidate with a good chance to win on strategic grounds, either to avoid "wasting" their votes on a sure loser in a multi-candidate race or because they view electoral strength in the spring as a portent of electability in the fall campaign. Then too, prospective voters uncertain about which is the "right" candidate for them may draw inferences from the behavior, whether already observed or merely anticipated, of their fellow voters; the logic here is, roughly, that "14,000 solid Iowans (probably) can't be wrong." Finally, the media's emphasis on the horse race may induce a horse race mentality in the minds of casual campaign-watchers, motivating them to "go with a winner" in much the same way that casual sports fans like to go with a winner in the Kentucky Derby; here complicated inferences about the candidate's underlying political qualities are irrelevant—the campaign is a game, and winning is what matters.

It is a difficult matter to untangle the motivations connecting prospective voters' expectations about who will win and their own preferences. None of the three explanations suggested here—strategic voting, cue-taking, or a simple desire to support a winner—seems sufficient by itself to account for the detailed patterns in the observed relationship. Probably all three, and perhaps others as well, are at work to different degrees for different people under different political circumstances. But for present purposes the important point is that, whatever the psychological mechanism, prospective voters' expectations about who will win the nomination do seem to have a significant impact on their own behavior.

The magnitude of that impact is evident in Figure 5.5, which shows how respondents' chances of supporting Hart in 1984 varied with their perceptions of his own chances of winning the nomination. The effect

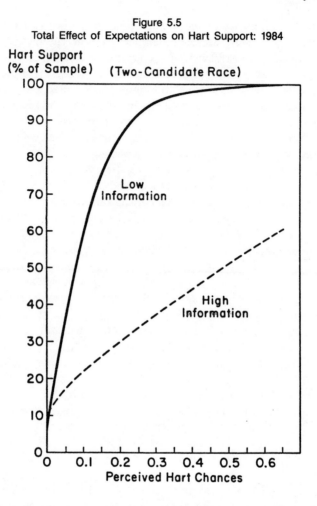

Figure 5.5
Total Effect of Expectations on Hart Support: 1984

of expectations is shown separately for two different information levels—
the average levels of information about Hart prevailing at the beginning
and end of the 1984 primary season. It appears from these results that
the impact of expectations on support for Hart was substantially greater
in the "Low Information" environment prevailing at the beginning of
the 1984 campaign, when he was relatively unknown, than in the "High
Information" environment prevailing at the end of the primary season.

Even at the end of the primary season the estimated effect of
expectations in Figure 5.5 is very considerable, with an increase of ten
percentage points in Hart's perceived chances producing an increase of
about eight percentage points in an average voter's probability of supporting him. But at the beginning of the campaign the apparent impact

of expectations is still more dramatic. Even relatively minor changes in expectations have very substantial effects; for example, an increase in Hart's perceived chances from ten percent to twenty percent would increase an average respondent's probability of supporting him by about 25 percentage points in the situation of relative uncertainty prevailing at the beginning of the campaign. For larger—but still plausible— variations in expectations, the same prospective voter can be virtually certain to oppose Hart or virtually certain to support him, simply depending on her perceptions of his chances.

The Limits of Momentum

The dynamic features of nominating campaigns described thus far— the impact of increasing information and improving expectations on public support—seem to leave little room for stalls or reversals in the upward-spiralling fortunes of a candidate with "Big Mo." But the history of recent campaigns suggests that such stalls and reversals are common, and that momentum alone is not enough to be nominated. Although Jimmy Carter in 1976 managed to survive "fuzziness," "ethnic purity," and Jerry Brown and went on to win the nomination against a divided field, the two candidates whose momentum pitted them against well-established front-runners both fell short. As Greenfield (1982, p. 42) wrote of George Bush's failure in 1980,

> the politics of momentum is a highly incomplete account of how Presidential politics works. It is an accurate account of a pattern that emerges with some frequency in an age of mass-media politics; but that pattern is by no means dominant, and is fully capable of being overwhelmed by other, more enduring political patterns. To put it most simply: there was never any reason to vote for George Bush for President. In premising his campaign on the factor of momentum, George Bush stripped his effort of any substantive or ideological rationale; and a campaign lacking such a rationale is almost impossible to sustain against a candidate who has labored long and hard to build a *political*, as opposed to a *strategic* case for his candidacy; which is what Ronald Reagan had been doing within the Republican Party for sixteen years.

The difficulty of sustaining a campaign premised on momentum arises from two related dynamic tendencies in the presidential nominating process. One of these tendencies has already been alluded to in my discussion of the role of expectations in the campaign. Although consequential at every stage, expectations matter most in situations where information is scarce—especially for relatively unknown candidates early in the primary season. Because increasing information eventually reduces the impact even of favorable expectations, "brush fires" of the sort ignited by Carter in 1976, Bush in 1980, and Hart in 1984 are to some extent self-extinguishing.

As the role of expectations fades with increasing information, there is a compensating tendency for underlying political considerations to play an increasingly important role in the nominating process. Prospective voters learn enough about an emerging candidate's political identity to weigh the "substantive or ideological rationale" for his campaign in the light of their own political values. In the absence of significant underlying political support, even a candidate with momentum on his side may fare poorly against an opponent who has "labored long and hard to build a *political*, as opposed to a *strategic* case for his candidacy."

This second dynamic pattern, of "political activation" (Bartels, 1988, p. 91), is evident in Figure 5.6, which shows the changing relationship between underlying predispositions toward Gary Hart and actual evaluations of Hart during the 1984 primary season.[8] There are some inexplicable variations in the relationship from week to week, but the widening gap between evaluations of Hart by respondents with pro-Hart predispositions and those with anti-Hart predispositions is clear. Before Super Tuesday those predisposed to oppose Hart evaluated him just as favorably as did those whose social and political characteristics made them predisposed to support him; but in the weeks after Super Tuesday, as information about Hart continued to accumulate, evaluations became increasingly accurate reflections of prospective voters' underlying political predispositions.[9]

The phenomenon of political activation appears in somewhat different form in Figure 5.7, which shows the estimated effect of predispositions toward Hart on choices between the two candidates for survey respondents at "Low" and "High" levels of information. As in Figure 5.5, "Low Information" represents the average level of information about Hart at the beginning of the 1984 primary season, before the Iowa caucuses. "High Information" represents the average level of information about Hart at the end of the primary season. Under both conditions it is clear that political predispositions did shape prospective voters' reactions to Hart; but they did so with considerably more force at the end of the campaign than at the beginning. At the beginning of the campaign, for example, survey respondents with college degrees supported Hart more than those with eighth-grade educations, but the difference amounted to less than five percentage points. By the end of the campaign the corresponding difference was about twelve percentage points.

Results like these suggest that presidential nominating campaigns, for all their emphasis on hoopla and horse race, do provide prospective

Figure 5.6
Predispositions and Evaluations of Hart: 1984

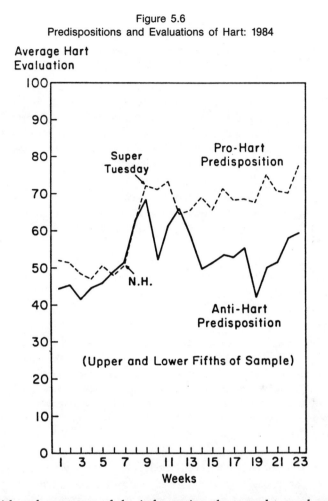

Average Hart
Evaluation

voters with at least some of the information they need to make political sense of the choices they face in the primary voting booth. The candidates' real political identities may not always matter from the start, in the first few weeks after an exciting new candidate like Carter, Bush, or Hart emerges from Iowa with momentum; but they matter in the end. The danger, from an institutional standpoint, is that by then it may be too late.

After Iowa:
Issues of Institutional Design

In many political systems, positions of party leadership are earned through decades of toil in the party organization. In contemporary

American politics the same positions can be seized—sometimes literally overnight—by candidates with negligible party credentials and very short histories as national political figures. In December 1974, James M. Perry recalled later (Moore and Fraser, 1977, p. 73),

> a Gallup poll asked voters to select their first choice for the [Democratic] nomination from a list of thirty-one names, including George Wallace, Hubert Humphrey, Henry Jackson, George McGovern, John Lindsay, Adlai Stevenson, Ralph Nader, Walter Mondale, on through Terry Sanford and Kevin White—but not including Jimmy Carter.

It is hard to imagine any other process of presidential selection that could produce a winner who, less than two years earlier, was not considered among the top thirty prospects for the job within his own party.

The dangers inherent in this remarkable openness have been noted repeatedly by critical observers. As Robert Scheer put it (Foley, Bitton, and Everett, 1980, p. 44),

> There's a special problem with the drawn out system of primaries and caucuses. What it allows is for an unknown to get in. These people do not have a track record. They don't have 12 years in the Senate and five in the House. They don't have things you can hang them with. You got a guy like Carter and you wrap him up, or get a guy like Caddell or Rafshoon wrapping him up, he doesn't have anything you can pin him on except some myths about what went on in Georgia. By the time you unravel that and find out some of the reality, the election is over anyway.

Obviously, one way to avoid getting nominees without track records would be to replace the sequential nominating process beginning in Iowa on Monday night with a national primary system. Carter, for one, would almost surely never have been nominated in a national primary. Without the momentum generated by the dynamics of the current system, only major contenders—candidates with substantial name recognition, financial support, and organizational resources—would have any real chance of winning.

A quasi-national primary of the sort that some observers see evolving on Super Tuesday would be a very different matter. With Iowa and New Hampshire still out in front, such a system would probably maximize the impact of small early victories on the subsequent course of the campaign. As David Broder (1986) put it, "The bigger the bloc of votes available the next Tuesday, the larger the premium for winning New Hampshire." But in a genuine national primary, Iowa and New Hampshire

TABLE 5.2   Hart's Projected Performance in One-Day National Primary, 1984 Democratic
Campaign

		Actual Hart %	National Primary	Difference
28 Feb	New Hampshire	37.3 (H)	28.2	9.1
6 Mar	Vermont	70.0 (H)	52.6 (H)	17.4
13 Mar	Alabama	20.7	8.1	12.6
	Florida	40.0 (H)	19.0	21.0
	Georgia	27.3	11.8	15.5
	Massachusetts	39.0 (H)	19.7	19.3
	Rhode Island	45.0 (H)	21.8	23.2
20 Mar	Illinois	35.2	17.2	18.0
27 Mar	Connecticut	52.6 (H)	31.3	21.3
3 Apr	New York	27.4	12.1	15.3
	Wisconsin	44.4 (H)	22.4	22.0
1 May	D.C.	7.1	2.5	4.6
	Tennessee	29.1	12.1	17.0
5 May	Louisiana	25.0	11.6	13.4
8 May	Indiana	41.8 (H)	19.0	22.8
	Maryland	24.3	9.6	14.7
	North Carolina	30.2	13.1	17.1
	Ohio	42.1 (H)	19.2	22.8
15 May	Nebraska	58.2 (H)	31.9	26.1
	Oregon	58.9 (H)	32.2	26.7
22 May	Idaho	58.0 (H)	31.9	26.1
5 Jun	California	41.2 (H)	18.9	22.3
	New Jersey	29.5	11.8	17.7
	New Mexico	46.5 (H)	22.2	24.3
	South Dakota	51.2 (H)	24.8	26.4
	West Virginia	37.1	15.0	22.1
	Mean	39.0	19.8	19.2

(H): Actual or projected Hart Victory.

Sources: Actual primary results; *Congressional Quarterly Weekly Report* and Orren (1985).
Projected national primary results; Author's calculations (Bartels 1988, Table 10.7).

would vote on the same day as every other state. There would be no opportunity for early demonstrations of public support, and thus no real possibility for unheralded candidates like Carter, Bush, and Hart to emerge from the pack.

The extent to which these candidates' successes depended on the sequential nature of the contemporary nominating process is suggested in Table 5.2, which provides projections of how Gary Hart might have done in 1984 in a one-day national primary. The projected results are based on a statistical analysis of the role of dynamic factors in determining actual state-by-state primary outcomes in the 1984 campaign (Bartels, 1988, pp. 247–267). By adjusting the actual primary outcomes to "correct" for dynamic effects of the sort considered earlier—for changes in levels of information, expectations, and political activation—I have attempted to estimate how Hart might have done if every state's primary had been held at the time of the Iowa caucuses in early February.[10]

The most striking thing about the projected results is how much of Hart's support in 1984 seems to have been attributable to the dynamics of the sequential primary system. In a one-day national primary, it appears, he would have received only about half as many votes as he actually did receive during the course of the primary season—and would have carried only one of the 27 primary states rather than fifteen. Hart's success in the later primaries appears from these projections to be attributable at least as much to momentum generated in Iowa and New Hampshire as to the underlying political support Hart brought to the 1984 campaign.[11]

Judgments about whether Hart should have come as close to being nominated as he did in 1984 must rest in part on judgments about the man himself. But at a more abstract level, it seems clear that the problem with the national primary solution is that it would preclude serious consideration of all newcomers, whether able and purposeful or shallow and dangerous. The openness of the existing sequential process, like many other salient features of real political systems, has both good and bad consequences. It sometimes forces primary voters to choose among unknown alternatives, but it also provides flexibility and opportunity.

The greatest failing of the existing process is that it works least well precisely when it is producing the virtues of openness—when an unknown candidate emerges in the early stages of a nominating campaign. That is when substantive political information is in short supply; that is when expectations about the "horse race"—expectations largely disconnected from substantive political considerations—play a crucial role in shaping the choices of prospective voters. And that is when reckless public enthusiasm could most easily produce an irrevocable mistake.

It seems clear that an ideal nominating process would somehow facilitate more informed decision making. Such a process would be sequential, but with sufficient time between events for the press and the public to absorb and reflect upon each new turn before coming to the next. Particularly in the early stages of the campaign, when the heat of momentum can be hottest, the process would minimize the likelihood of unstoppable brush fires for candidates wrapped up in myths.

This line of argument suggests that one crucial parameter of institutional design in the contemporary nominating process is the frequency of events relative to the speed at which the public learns about the candidates' real political identities. Once a bandwagon begins to roll, how long does it take the press and the public to recover their bearings and begin to evaluate a new candidate critically, as a political leader rather than as a media star? Obviously, we have no clear, precise answer to that question; but some relevant evidence does exist.

For one thing, a comparison of the experiences of George Bush in 1980 and Gary Hart in 1984 is suggestive. When Bush upset Reagan in Iowa, he became "the hottest property in American politics" (Cannon and Peterson, 1980, p. 137). But in the month separating the Iowa caucuses and the New Hampshire primary his momentum fizzled, and he lost in New Hampshire by a substantial margin. Hart emerged by finishing a distant second to Walter Mondale in Iowa in 1984, and parlayed his momentum into a big win in New Hampshire one week later, followed in rapid succession by additional victories in primaries and caucuses in Vermont, Maine, and Wyoming in the next ten days. Hart's bandwagon only began to slow on Super Tuesday—three weeks after his original emergence in Iowa. There are of course, a variety of explanations for these contrasting patterns of events. But one worth considering is that the "shelf life" of momentum in its most intense and uncritical form may be no more than two or three weeks.

My own analyses, though by no means conclusive, are consistent with the notion that a period of three weeks or so between key events may provide a critical "cooling off" period after an early-season surprise. Most notably, the changing relationship between predispositions toward Hart and evaluations of him, shown in Figure 5.7, suggests that about three weeks are required for prospective voters to begin to sort out what a new candidate is about and how his political views and values measure up to their own. Similar lags appeared in the public's familiarity with Hart's specific issue stands and character traits relative to their willingness to make overall judgments about him (Bartels, 1988, pp. 63–66), and in the extent to which perceptions of Hart's issue positions reflected political reality rather than projections onto him of their own policy preferences (Bartels, 1988, pp. 105–107).

A saner primary calendar, with key events separated by longer opportunities for learning and reflection, could probably only be established through legislation; the political parties are not sufficiently centralized to impose any orderly system on unwilling state affiliates. But once established, such a calendar might go some way toward mitigating the dangers inherent in the dynamics of the current system, while preserving the flexibility and openness that make the current system more attractive than the most obvious alternative, a one-day national primary.

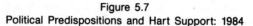

Figure 5.7
Political Predispositions and Hart Support: 1984

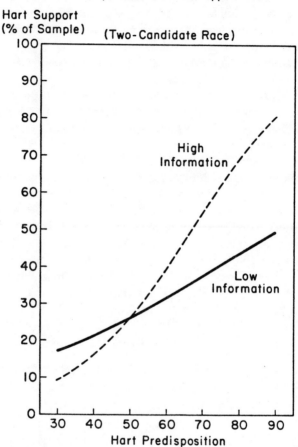

What is at stake is the capacity of the nominating process to facilitate sober political evaluation. Richard Leone, a Mondale campaign adviser (quoted by Moore, 1986, pp. 71–72), recalled after the 1984 election that his candidate's hopes in the dark days after Hart's New Hampshire upset rested on just this sort of sober evaluation—on the possibility that

> the degree of positive television coverage, the intensity of media hype about Hart, and the necessarily shallow nature of his support, since people were moving to him in droves and knew very little about him at a very early stage, would inevitably lead to a reconsideration—who is this person who has suddenly been thrust into the forefront? . . . [P]eople would

wake up the next morning and wonder whom they had spent the night with and start to think about what it all meant.

In 1984, the reconsideration did come in time for Mondale to survive and eventually win the nomination. But it was a near-run thing. A less precarious nominating process would retain the opportunity for a candidate like Hart to emerge into prominence, but also give prospective voters a little more time to "wake up the next morning" and consider their choices in the cool light of day.

Postscript: The 1988 Campaign

The events of 1988 provide new opportunities to test propositions advanced here and elsewhere about the role of Iowa in the contemporary presidential nominating process.[12] Although data adequate to test such propositions in detail are not yet available for the 1988 campaign, the broad outlines of available aggregate poll results seem, for the most part, to be consistent with the storyline set out above.[13]

Both Gallup and CBS News conducted polls of each party's registered voters in New Hampshire in January—before the Iowa caucuses—and then again in the week after Iowa. The results from both polls, which were very similar, are shown in Table 5.3. On the Democratic side the Iowa winner, Richard Gephardt, gained about ten percentage points in New Hampshire—a gain almost exactly consistent in magnitude with that estimated for Gary Hart in 1984 in Table 5.2 above. Support for each of the other major Democratic candidates remained essentially unchanged in both polls. On the Republican side the Iowa winner, Robert Dole, also gained about ten percentage points in New Hampshire, while George Bush, who finished an embarrassing third in Iowa, lost a similar amount. Pat Robertson, who stunned the press by finishing second, gained about six percentage points in New Hampshire, while Jack Kemp, who finished fourth, lost about four percentage points.

As it turned out, neither Gephardt nor Dole was able to parlay his success in Iowa into a major victory in New Hampshire—or anywhere else.[14] In Dole's case the virtual dead heat in New Hampshire reflected in the later Gallup and CBS News polls in Table 5.3 slipped away in the final days of the campaign, and Bush's victory in New Hampshire helped him hold on to a substantial lead in the southern Super Tuesday states. What would have happened in the South if Dole had beat Bush in New Hampshire? That is one of the most interesting might-have-beens of the 1988 campaign. But the apparent magnitude of Dole's momentum coming out of Iowa suggests that a second highly publicized victory in New Hampshire might have helped him cut substantially into

TABLE 5.3   The Effect of Iowa on New Hampshire, 1988

Democrats

	Iowa Vote	Gallup Poll 8-10 Jan	12-13 Feb	Change
Gephardt	31.3	5	18	+13%
Simon	26.7	12	14	+ 2%
Dukakis	22.1	39	42	+ 3%
Jackson	8.8	5	6	+ 1%
Gore	0	4	4	-------
		(N=416)	(N=1177)	

	Iowa Vote	CBS News Poll 25-30 Jan	9-15 Feb	Change
Gephardt	31.3	7	16	+ 9%
Simon	26.7	16	14	- 2%
Dukakis	22.1	40	39	- 1%
Jackson	8.8	6	6	-------
Gore	0	4	5	+ 1%
		(N=434)	(N=2396)	

Republicans

	Iowa Vote	Gallup Poll 8-10 Jan	12-13 Feb	Change
Dole	37.3	23	33	+10%
Robertson	24.6	4	11	+ 7%
Bush	18.6	38	28	-10%
Kemp	11.1	15	12	- 3%
		(N=545)	(N=1531)	

	Iowa Vote	CBS News Poll 25-30 Jan	9-15 Feb	Change
Dole	37.3	20	30	+10%
Robertson	24.6	4	9	+ 5%
Bush	18.6	42	32	-10%
Kemp	11.1	16	11	- 5%
		(N=513)	(N=2820)	

Sources: Iowa caucus results: *Congressional Quarterly Weekly Report*.
            Poll results: Gallup and CBS News press releases.

Bush's southern support, despite the vice president's significant political resources of familiarity, organization, and incumbency.

Gephardt was the less well known of the Iowa winners, and thus the best-positioned candidate to be the "new political star" of the 1988 campaign. The advantage of being a relative unknown does seem to be reflected in Gephardt's "Iowa bounce," which was similar in magnitude to the one Dole got from a bigger and more dramatic win. But Gephardt had trouble competing for media attention with the clearer and more "newsworthy" story on the Republican side.[15] Gephardt's ability to capitalize on momentum from Iowa was also limited by the relative narrowness of his issue base,[16] and by charges of opportunism and inconsistency levelled immediately by the press and the other candidates. Finally, Gephardt was not helped by the primary calendar: unlike Hart in 1984, for whom New Hampshire was an excellent state in which to keep his momentum building, Gephardt in New Hampshire had to compete on the home turf of his strongest opponent, Michael Dukakis.

The fact that neither of the Iowa winners could parlay his post-caucus momentum into real success in the rest of the campaign has led some commentators to downplay the likely significance of the Iowa caucuses in future nominating contests. They argue that if Super Tuesday survives in its present form, or expands even further, candidates will increasingly treat the preliminary events in Iowa and New Hampshire as just that—preliminaries. But the actual course of the 1988 campaign, both on Super Tuesday and thereafter, seems to belie this reasoning.

Gallup poll results from the South, shown in the top half of Table 5.4, suggest that Gephardt and Dole each gained about five percentage points in the region from the combined effect of Iowa and New Hampshire. Dole's problems were that Bush began the campaign with a two-to-one lead in the South, and that Dole himself seemed to sour after Bush's successful comeback in New Hampshire. Gephardt's major difficulty was that Dukakis's clear win in New Hampshire, even as a virtual favorite son, made him an even bigger gainer in the South. Dukakis went from 8 percent to 25 percent in the southern polls, an increase that translates into almost 1.3 million votes (out of 7.5 million cast) in the southern primary states on Super Tuesday. By contrast, the candidate who ignored Iowa and New Hampshire (or at least loudly proclaimed that strategy after failing to attract much support), Albert Gore, gained exactly one percent.[17] The rest, as they say, is history.

If the results from the South provide little incentive for candidates to downplay Iowa and New Hampshire, the same is true of the national poll results from CBS News shown in the bottom half of Table 5.4. Dukakis gained about fifteen points in the national standings in the month of Iowa and New Hampshire, Gephardt about eight, and Dole about five (in spite of Bush's New Hampshire comeback); support for the other candidates remained relatively unchanged. These results from the 1988 campaign reinforce the conclusion I drew earlier based on the experience of previous primary seasons: that a further increase in the number of primaries held on Super Tuesday "would probably maximize the impact of small early victories on the subsequent course of the campaign."

144

TABLE 5.4   The Effect of Iowa and New Hampshire on the South and the Nation, 1988

The South

	Avg. Vote[a]	Gallup Poll 15-17 Jan	19-21 Feb	Change
Dukakis	29.0	8	25	+17%
Gephardt	25.6	6	11	+ 2%
Simon	21.9	5	6	+ 1%
Jackson	8.3	21	18	- 3%
Gore	3.4	17	18	+ 1%
		(N=370)	(N=426)	

	Avg. Vote[a]	Gallup Poll 15-17 Jan	19-21 Feb	Change
Dole	32.8	25	31	+ 6%
Bush	28.1	54	54	-------
Robertson	17.0	7	9	+ 2%
Kemp	12.0	5	3	- 2%
		(N=322)	(N=333)	

The Nation

	Avg. Vote[a]	Gallup Poll 15-17 Jan	19-21 Feb	Change
Dukakis	29.0	6	21	+15%
Gephardt	25.6	4	12	+ 8%
Simon	21.9	9	6	- 3%
Jackson	8.3	17	13	- 4%
Gore	3.4	4	8	+ 4%
		(N=602)	(N=933)	

	Avg. Vote[a]	Gallup Poll 15-17 Jan	19-21 Feb	Change
Dole	32.8	22	27	+ 5%
Bush	28.1	41	42	+ 1%
Robertson	17.0	7	7	-------
Kemp	12.0	4	3	- 1%
		(N=438)	(N=684)	

[a]Avg. Vote is the average of each candidate's vote shares in the Iowa caucus and the New Hampshire primary.

Sources: Iowa caucus and New Hampshire primary results: *Congressional Quarterly Weekly Report*. Poll results: Gallup and CBS News press releases.

Iowa, it seems, may continue to have its moments in the sun.

Notes

This chapter is based on my book, *Presidential Primaries and the Dynamics of Public Choice* (Princeton University Press, 1988). Readers wanting more extended treatments of the issues raised will find them there. The chapter was prepared during a fellowship year at the Center for Advanced Study in the Behavioral Sciences. I am grateful to the Center, the National Science Foundation, and the University of Rochester for financial support, and to my colleagues and friends— most notably Henry E. Brady—for stimulation, insight, and encouragement.

1. This apt description was offered by one of Bush's chief rivals in the 1980 campaign, Howard Baker.

2. In 1984, party rules called for about fifteen percent of the seats at the Democratic convention to be reserved for congressmen chosen by their colleagues outside the public delegate-selection process. These "super delegates," selected before the first primaries and caucuses, provided much of Mondale's eventual delegate cushion. Mondale also benefited from the failure of the Hart organization, intent on surviving the early contests in Iowa and New Hampshire, to file full delegate slates for some of the later primaries.

3. Except where otherwise noted, all of the analysis in this paper is based on survey data from the 1984 National Election Study conducted by the University of Michigan's Center for Political Studies. For my purposes the relevant data consist of 868 interviews, averaging approximately 40 minutes in duration and spread roughly evenly over the 23 weeks of the primary campaign from mid-January to mid-June, with Democratic party identifiers or "leaners." The data and supporting documentation describing the study design and procedures are available through the Inter-University Consortium for Political and Social Research.

4. The form of the familiarity measure available in the 1984 NES survey is somewhat different from that available for other campaigns. Respondents were not asked directly whether they "knew anything about" the candidates, but were invited to rate on a general "feeling thermometer" any candidate whose name they said they recognized. Thus, the proportions shown in Figure 5.1 represent respondents who recognized and were willing to rate Mondale, Hart, and Askew. Being willing to rate a candidate is not obviously equivalent to claiming to know something about him; but detailed comparisons in cases where both measures are available suggest that differences due to question wording are on the order of one to three percent.

5. The estimated levels of information about Hart and Mondale shown in Figure 5.2 are based on a threshold model of the survey response similar to the model employed for analyzing issue perceptions in Bartels (1986). Because the model allows for a step increase in information about Hart after New Hampshire but not after Iowa, the figure probably understates somewhat the amount of learning about Hart that occurred in the week between Iowa and New Hampshire and overstates somewhat the amount that occurred in the first

week after Hart's New Hampshire primary victory (Bartels, 1988, pp. 327–328, 338–339).

6. The 1984 National Election Study survey asked respondents to rate each candidate's chances of winning the nomination on a scale running from zero ("no chance") to 100 ("certain victory"). These ratings resist interpretation as probability estimates in any literal sense. For example, the average respondent assigned the six candidates in the survey a total "probability" of winning the nomination of more than two hundred percent. I have rescaled the raw ratings in an effort to approximate more closely a genuine probability measure (Bartels, 1988, pp. 321–323). In addition, since the "chances" question was not asked for Gary Hart before the New Hampshire primary, I have simulated expectations about Hart's chances in the first seven weeks of the primary season; fortunately, the results reported below do not appear to be particularly sensitive to this reconstruction of missing data.

7. It is also likely that individual voters' expectations about the race are, in part, projections of their own preferences (Berelson, Lazarsfeld, and McPhee, 1954, p. 289; Bartels, 1985). In 1984 those respondents most predisposed to oppose Mondale were also most favorably impressed by Hart's chances of winning the nomination.

8. By "predispositions" I mean the complex of political and social characteristics that were systematically related to evaluations of Hart among those survey respondents who knew the most about him (Bartels, 1987; 1988, pp. 84–86). The "pro-Hart" responses in Figure 5.6 are from the fifth of the Democratic sample whose characteristics made them most predisposed to support Hart; the "anti-Hart" responses focus on the fifth of the sample whose characteristics made them least predisposed to support Hart. Favorable predispositions toward Hart were concentrated among well-educated, young, white, non-Jewish, non-union respondents with liberal political views. Favorable predispositions toward Walter Mondale were concentrated among the traditional elements of the New Deal coalition: liberals, Jews, blacks, union members, older people, and strongly partisan Democrats.

9. The same pattern is evident in the relationship between underlying predispositions toward Walter Mondale and evaluations of Mondale. Throughout the campaign, differences in evaluations of Mondale attributable to underlying political predispositions were greater than those shown for Hart in Figure 5.6, as one would expect from the fact that Mondale was better known than Hart. But even for Mondale, substantive political considerations became an increasingly important determinant of public reactions to his candidacy as information about him accumulated from week to week.

10. Clearly, any simulation of this sort will fail to account for some of the consequences of a real national primary system. In 1984, it is likely that Hart would not even have bothered to run had the prospect of generating momentum in Iowa and New Hampshire been closed off. In this sense the projections in Table 5.2 probably underestimate the true impact of the sequential primary system on the nature and outcome of the nominating process.

11. The sequential primary system is a major boon to any relatively unknown candidate who manages, like Hart in 1984, to emerge from Iowa with momentum. Nevertheless, it is worth noting that Hart was particularly advantaged by the specific sequence of state primaries in 1984. The first two primary states, New Hampshire and Vermont, provided remarkably fertile ground for a Hart bandwagon. Neither has an appreciable number of blacks, a group Hart has never succeeded in winning over. Neither is heavily urbanized. And both were notable strongholds of John Anderson's independent campaign in 1980—a campaign whose message and constituency overlapped significantly with Hart's in 1984. To have these two states at the beginning of the primary calendar, following almost immediately upon Hart's emergence in Iowa, at the height of media and public interest in the campaign, and with Hart himself a virtually blank slate on which voters could project their own pictures of an ideal candidate, was a remarkable stroke of good luck.

12. The preceding sections were written in January 1988 for the Shambaugh Conference and appear here with only slight editing. This postscript was written in July 1988, after the end of the primary season.

13. The preliminary analyses in this section are based on results from Gallup and CBS News polls conducted during the 1988 primary season. I am grateful to Gallup and CBS News for providing these results, and to Stanley Presser for arranging access to them. More careful and exhaustive analyses of these data and those from other sources, including the 1988 National Election Study Super Tuesday survey, will, I hope, follow in due course.

14. Both won in South Dakota one week after the New Hampshire primary, but those victories received relatively little attention. Gephardt also won on Super Tuesday in his home state, Missouri; but otherwise both were shut out for the remainder of the primary season, and both quit the race in late March.

15. Gephardt's ill fortune was already evident on the night of his caucus victory, when CBS News devoted the first twenty minutes of election night coverage almost entirely to Dole, Robertson, and Bush; Gephardt was interviewed briefly toward the end of the show. The next day's National Edition of the New York Times had the Republican results in a front page headline; the story by E. J. Dionne, Jr., based on results from two-thirds of the precincts, included a single sentence mentioning that "there were no similarly conclusive results from the Democratic caucuses." During the next week, four of five New Hampshire Republicans in the CBS News poll knew that Dole had won in Iowa; less than two of three New Hampshire Democrats knew that Gephardt had won.

16. 38 percent of Gephardt's supporters in a CBS News Iowa exit poll mentioned farm policy as one of the two issues that mattered most in deciding their votes, while a third mentioned trade or the problem of "notch babies"; the corresponding percentages among supporters of the other candidates were less than half as large.

17. Gore picked up another ten to twelve percent between the time of the second Gallup poll and the Super Tuesday primaries, mostly on the strength of an expensive television advertising campaign, while Dukakis dropped about two percent.

148   Larry M. Bartels

References

Bartels, Larry M. 1985. Expectations and Preferences in Presidential Nominating Campaigns. *American Political Science Review*, 79: 804–815.

———. 1986. Issue Voting Under Uncertainty: An Empirical Test. *American Journal of Political Science*, 30: 709–728.

———. 1988. *Presidential Primaries and the Dynamics of Public Choice*. Princeton: Princeton University Press.

Berelson, Bernard R., Paul F. Lazarsfeld, and William N. McPhee. 1954. *Voting: A Study of Opinion Formation in a Presidential Campaign*. Chicago: University of Chicago Press.

Brady, Henry E., and Richard Johnston. 1987. What's the Primary Message: Horse Race or Issue Journalism? In Gary R. Orren and Nelson W. Polsby, eds., *Media and Momentum*. Chatham, NJ: Chatham House.

Broder, David. March 12, 1986. The Southern Primary: Another Mistake. *Washington Post*.

Cannon, Lou, and William Peterson. 1980. GOP. In Richard Harwood, ed., *The Pursuit of the Presidency 1980*. New York: Berkley Books.

Foley, John, Dennis A. Britton, and Eugene B. Everett, Jr., eds. 1980. *Nominating a President: The Process and the Press*. New York: Praeger.

Greenfield, Jeff. 1982. *The Real Campaign: How the Media Missed the Story of the 1980 Campaign*. New York: Summit Books.

Moore, David. 1985. The Death of Politics in New Hampshire. In Michael J. Robinson and Austin Ranney, eds., *The Mass Media in Campaign '84: Articles from Public Opinion Magazine*. Washington, DC: American Enterprise Institute.

Moore, Jonathan, ed. 1986. *Campaign for President: The Managers Look at '84*. Dover, MA: Auburn House.

———, and Janet Fraser, eds., 1977. *Campaign for President: The Managers Look at '76*. Cambridge, MA: Ballinger.

Orren, Gary R. 1985. The Nomination Process: Vicissitudes of Candidate Selection. In Michael Nelson, ed., *The Elections of 1984*. Washington, DC: Congressional Quarterly Press.

Patterson, Thomas E. 1980. *The Mass Media Election: How Americans Choose Their President*. New York: Praeger.

Robinson, Michael J., and Maura Clancey. 1985. Teflon Politics. In Michael J. Robinson and Austin Ranney, eds., *The Mass Media in Campaign '84: Articles from Public Opinion Magazine*. Washington, DC: American Enterprise Institute.

———, and Margaret A. Sheehan. 1983. *Over the Wire and On TV*. New York: Russell Sage Foundation.

Schram, Martin. 1977. *Running for President 1976: The Carter Campaign*. New York: Stein and Day.

WGBH. 1984. So You Want to Be President. (FRONTLINE transcript #216). Boston: WGBH Transcripts.

Witcover, Jules. 1977. *Marathon: The Pursuit of the Presidency 1972–1976*. New York: New American Library.

6

The Iowa Caucuses in a Front-Loaded System: A Few Historical Lessons

Nelson W. Polsby

In 1988, Iowa selected 52 Democratic delegates and 37 Republican delegates to their respective national party conventions, 1.2 percent of all Democratic delegates and 1.4 percent of all Republican delegates. Iowa's small size notwithstanding, the initial stage of the selection process, the February 8 precinct caucuses, received highly attentive media coverage, very much in keeping with the extraordinary attention these caucuses have received in previous years. In 1984, according to an actual count of news coverage appearing on all three television networks plus in the *New York Times*, Iowa, with 2.5 percent of the U.S. population, received 12.8 percent of the total news coverage accorded the presidential race from January to June (Adams, 1987, pp. 42–59).

Owing to the hospitality of the University of Iowa Political Science Department, in February, 1988 a few political scientists had the pleasure of actually going to Iowa and watching the caucus of the Democratic party of the 4th precinct of Johnson County, 289 or 287 strong, depending on the count you use, all gathered together in the auditorium of the Lincoln School of Iowa City, Iowa. Before the Democrats got their act together on the evening of February 8, it was possible to observe the 4th Precinct Republican meeting—in the Lincoln School's kindergarten room, as it happens. There they were, about 60 Republicans, sitting decorously on those tiny little kindergarten chairs, chatting quietly and behaving just as though they were waiting for a string quartet concert to begin. The Democrats, true to form, put on a noisier and more cheerfully disorderly show of selecting 9 delegates to the Johnson county caucus of the Democratic party a month hence. The county caucus would send delegates to the congressional district convention a month after that, and they in turn elected delegates to the Iowa state convention who sent delegates to the national convention of the Democratic party in July. These complications alone justified the view that the fortunes of Presidential hopefuls were as flotsam on a roiling sea of process.

At least on the Democratic side, the Iowa precinct caucuses had something directly to do with the actual selection of actual delegates to the national convention. On the Republican side, the numbers breathlessly reported on the networks were the outcome of a straw poll ballot, conducted at the precinct caucuses, and phoned into the networks just like the real delegate divisions on the Democratic side. After the straw poll was conducted, Republican delegates to the next level up were selected in each precinct, without any necessary connection to the straw poll.

As David Oman, co-chairman of the Iowa Republican party, described the process the week before to the *Presidential Campaign Hotline*:

> Essentially we have one very large straw poll taken in 2500 different locations simultaneously. . . . Those at the caucus will be given small cards and will mark on these cards their choice for president. The cards will be tallied. . . .
> Our straw poll is not tied to the process of choosing delegates. After the poll is taken and reported, the caucus will then pick its precinct committeeman and committeewoman, then pick the men and women who will go to the Republican county convention, and then discuss the platform.[1]

The county conventions met in March and picked delegates to congressional district conventions, which met in June on the eve of the state convention. The district conventions selected three national convention delegates for each district and then the state convention selected the rest. Thus the straw poll might or might not predict the results of the delegate selection process accurately in any given year. In 1988, the preferences of the eventual delegates were 16 for Dole, 12 for Bush, two each for Robertson and Kemp, and five uncommitted.[2]

On the Democratic side, the caucuses are more immediately consequential. As Phil Roeder, Communications Director of the Iowa State Democratic Party described it ahead of time to the *Hotline*:

> at 7:30 PM on caucus night in 2489 precincts people will start to break into candidate preference groups. . . . They will physically divide into different groups for each candidate and in most instances there is an uncommitted group as well.[3]

These groups elect delegates according to the number of delegates each precinct was entitled to by virtue of its population. Preference groups were allocated delegates depending on what proportion of the people who showed up to the caucus were in each group. Groups that were too small to receive delegates had the option of breaking up and their members could migrate to their second choices or to the uncommitted group, or they could seek as a group to combine with one or more other small groups so as to be eligible to receive a delegate. Each of the groups then selected their delegates to the county convention. Democratic delegates selected in this fashion were, unlike the Republican delegates, usually pledged to a Presidential candidate as they moved up through the county and district conventions to the state convention.

Given the complications in ascertaining what the actual outcome of the precinct caucuses is, it is a wonder that there is so much news media coverage of the Iowa caucuses. Nevertheless, the coverage is there, because the Iowa caucuses are, in effect, the gateway to a long and complex nomination process, and all players and all observers very much want whatever information they can glean from the Iowa precinct caucuses if only to position themselves for the next round. The media need to know to whom to give special attention. Financial supporters of various candidates want to know whether it is worthwhile to continue to give, or to steer, money to their first choices or whether it is time to jump to other alternatives. Voters want to know which candidacies are viable, which futile.[4]

Thus, out of all the possible objects of study in the three ring circus of the American presidential nominating process, the grounds for paying special attention to the Iowa caucuses are that the system as a whole is conspicuously front-loaded, and Iowa is furthest to the front. The purpose of this short essay will be to review our understanding of what it means logically and strategically to have a front-loaded nomination process and to examine historically the effects of the Iowa caucuses on the fortunes of presidential candidates.

The temptation to ignore history is ever-present. Each quadrennial nomination sequence has plenty of elements of uniqueness, and our entire historical experience of Presidential elections yields very few instances at best. So underlying this discussion is what readers may wish to view as a pedagogic preference for attempting to extract the lessons of history even though we must acknowledge that contemporary actors are not necessarily bound to act in accordance with them.

Even further constraining a historical view is the fact that whatever happened before the drastic changes of the post-1968 reforms should probably be ignored on the grounds that the system overall was fundamentally altered by these reforms. It is the reforms that front-loaded the presidential nominating process.[5] Consequently, considering evidence from 1968 and before is bound to be drastically misleading as a guide to the structural constraints and strategic opportunities that shape the choices of contemporary actors. So we are left, in effect, with exactly eight historical data points, four Democratic, four Republican, representing the elections of 1972, 1976, 1980 and 1984. And these, owing to the effects of incumbency, can be reduced even further.

1972. In 1972 the Iowa caucuses were for the first time set early in the year, on January 24. This date was arrived at because the Democratic state convention was to be held on May 20 owing to the availability on that date of a suitable hall. Working backward from May 20, adequate time had to be provided to prepare for each of the earlier stages of the process, and the entire sequence had to be completed within the same calendar year as the national convention. Thus the January date (Apple, 1988).[6]

In 1972, the Republican incumbent, Richard Nixon, had only token opposition in Iowa from two Representatives in Congress, Paul (Pete) McCloskey of California on his left and John Ashbrook of Ohio on his right.

The Democratic caucuses, on the other hand, were quite important. After the incident at Chappaquiddick Island in the summer of 1969 immobilized Edward Kennedy as a factor in presidential election politics, it was assumed by most observers that the Democratic party's 1968 Vice-Presidential candidate, Senator Edmund S. Muskie, of Maine, would be the nominee. During 1971 Muskie led all Democrats in the public opinion polls and, indeed, beat President Nixon in trial heats.[7] But operating under obsolete strategic premises, Muskie failed to announce his candidacy until January 4, 1972. The assumption under the old dispensation was that only weak candidates announced early and willingly subjected themselves to the rigors of early campaigning. Presumably, weak candidates had no choice. The task of weak candidates was by their early activity to demonstrate unexpected popularity so as to change the minds of party leaders who otherwise would not support them. Thus an early start was necessary for candidates who had nothing to lose by risking early disappointment. Strong candidates waited, and collected endorsements from the party notables whose good opinion had, in the past, readily translated into solid delegate support at the national convention from state party delegations that these party leaders influenced or controlled.

In April, 1971, Muskie's campaign director Berl Bernhard said (Muskie Campaign: Cautious Pace By the Man in Front, 1971, p. 857):

> There's no real necessity to [announce early]. . . . When you do it, you should be ready to do a bit more than just announce. You do it to maximize your position; you don't do it just for the ritual. The announcement is

the clarion call to people who want to work for you to get ready. The most important thing Ed Muskie can do right now, rather than announce, is to talk about substantive issues.

As of that month, Richard H. Stewart, Muskie's press secretary, said (May and Fraser, 1973, p. 35):

I thought Muskie was in awfully good shape. The money was flowing in fairly well in keeping with Muskie's standing in the polls. I figured that all we had to do was sit and wait, and that it was only a matter of a few months before Muskie would win the nomination. . . .

By the time the Muskie organization woke up to the fact that what was required was state by state campaigning to win the popular support of a loyal Muskie faction of voters, it was much too late. George McGovern, whose initial standing in the public opinion trial heats was negligible, out-organized Muskie in most early states, which is to say he put together an enthusiastic group of die-hard workers mobilized around anti-war sentiment. Neither McGovern nor Muskie invested much effort in Iowa. The next day the newspapers reported unofficially, with incomplete returns, that Muskie beat McGovern in the precinct caucuses in Iowa 35.5 percent to 22.6 percent, with 35.8 percent uncommitted. The unexpected closeness of this margin pushed Muskie into overwork and an unaccustomed public display of emotional behavior in front of the building housing the offices of the *Manchester Union Leaders* in New Hampshire.[8] By the time the news media analysts were finished with the New Hampshire results, prior "expectations" that the U.S. Senator from a neighboring state should win an overwhelming victory—over 50 percent—completely dominated the fact that Muskie had in fact won once again (46 percent to 37 percent). Because his win was 4 or 5 points less impressive than "expected," Muskie support—especially financial support—began to dry up, and he withdrew from the race altogether by April 27.

The Muskie presidency was nibbled to death by ducks before it began. This extraordinary spectacle gave unmistakable evidence of the fact that changing the rules had changed the game. Pre-convention skirmishes were no longer simply important evidence to be taken into account by party leaders in making nominations: they were the contest itself.

Iowa did not administer the coup de grace to Muskie: that happened in New Hampshire. At most what happened in Iowa energized the participants in the New Hampshire primary and structured the alternatives for New Hampshire voters.

1976. Once again an incumbent was running on the Republican side. This time, however, Gerald Ford was the incumbent. Ford had never been a Republican presidential nominee and he was not an eloquent defender of his presidency. He was faced by a serious challenge from Ronald Reagan. Iowa came out in a dead heat between the two; both ended up with 18 delegates to the national convention. Ford won the official straw poll the night of the precinct caucuses, but by only a small margin. R.W. Apple (1976) of the *New York Times* characterized the Republican effort in Iowa by both candidates as "all but invisible, with only marginal organizational efforts by the supporters of Mr. Ford and Mr. Reagan."

On the Democratic side, the candidate who focused hardest on Iowa was Jimmy Carter. Hamilton Jordan, Carter's campaign manager, put together a strategy that was exactly three events deep, requiring strong showings in Iowa and New Hampshire, and a careful positioning as the anti-Wallace Southerner in the Florida primary.[9] The Carter strategy dovetailed nicely with those of his main competitors. Henry Jackson's campaign was designed to start late: a token effort in Iowa (January 19) and New Hampshire (February 24) followed by an unequivocal win in Massachusetts (March 2), only a week later. After all, Massachusetts' 104 delegates greatly exceeded the Iowa–New Hampshire combination of 64. Thus Jackson's decision to play from "strength" (Drew, 1977, Witcover, 1977).

Morris Udall's campaign was strategically incoherent. First Udall made an effort in Iowa, then, in an attempt to stretch his resources to cover as many primaries as possible (there were 30 Democratic primaries in 1976) Udall's campaign slackened its Iowa effort. As news coverage focused even more strongly on Iowa, however, Udall at the last minute recommitted resources to the race (Witcover, 1977, pp. 202–205; Drew, 1977; Schram, 1977, pp. 13–15). He was too late. Although he finished as high as second in seven primaries in 1976, in Iowa Udall came in fifth with 5.9 percent of the vote behind uncommitted with 37 percent of the caucus vote, Jimmy Carter with 28 percent, Birch Bayh with 13 percent, and Fred Harris with 10 percent.

The next day, R.W. Apple minimized the strong uncommitted sentiment and created the first major instance in which the Iowa caucuses combined importantly with mass media spin to launch a presidential candidacy. His story on the front page of the *New York Times* read (Apple, 1976):

Former Governor Jimmy Carter of Georgia scored an impressive victory in yesterday's Iowa Democratic precinct caucuses, demonstrating strength among rural, blue-collar, black, and suburban voters.

Mr. Carter defeated his closest rival, Senator Birch Bayh of Indiana, by a margin of more than 2–1, and left his other four challengers far behind. The uncommitted vote, which many Iowa politicians had forecast at more than 50 percent, amounted to only about a third of the total, slightly more than that of Mr. Carter.[10]

This article, with its strong and coherent story line, cast a long shadow. It contained many elements that in later years would worry journalists— notably the use of such a word as "impressive" (to whom?) in the lead of what ostensibly was a news story and the belittling of the uncommitted vote because of the disappointed "forecasts" or expectations of anonymous politicians.

Elizabeth Drew's (1977, p. 16) diary for the day after the Iowa caucuses said:

This morning, Carter, who managed to get to New York on time, was interviewed on the CBS Morning News, the Today Show and ABC's Good Morning America also ran segments on Carter. On the CBS Evening News, Walter Cronkite said that the Iowa voters have spoken "and for the Democrats what they said was 'Jimmy Carter.'"

This coverage set the stage for New Hampshire, where Carter alone ran as a centrist Democrat and received 28.4 percent of the vote. Although he filed a slate of delegates, Jackson sat the primary out, and no fewer than four candidates, Udall (at 22.7 percent), Sargent Shriver (at 8.2 percent), Fred Harris (at 10.8 percent), and Birch Bayh (at 15.2 percent) divided the liberal Democratic vote.

1980. By 1980, it was beginning to be understood that there was no such thing as a successful presidential strategy that ignored early delegate selection events. President Carter's managers worked hard to structure the order in which states selected delegates so as to maximize favorable publicity impact, seeking to move southern primaries up to the head of the line (Polsby, 1981, pp. 47–48). Carter, aided by a rally round the flag at the start of the Iranian hostage crisis, beat Edward Kennedy in Iowa 59.1 percent to 31.2 percent. Iowa momentum helped Carter amass a majority of delegates far more quickly in 1980 than he had done in 1976 (Polsby, 1981, p. 49).

On the Republican side, Iowa nearly did the front-runner, Ronald Reagan, in. Saving his energy, Reagan campaigned only 8 days in the state and passed up the major all-candidate Republican debate. Caucus turnout on the Republican side jumped to 110,000 participants from a mere 22,000 in 1976. Howard Baker, an interested party, remarked that the Iowa caucuses had become "the functional equivalent of a primary."

George Bush edged Reagan 31.5 percent to 29.4 percent in the straw vote, and as Jack Germond and Jules Witcover (1981, p. 96) observed, the Iowa caucuses served in 1980 to clear "the underbrush of candidates with little future . . . establishing a definite pecking order among those who remained."

Only a drastic change of strategy (including the replacement of John Sears, the strategist) and some extraordinarily vigorous propagandizing by the *Manchester Union Leader* saved Ronald Reagan's bacon by aiding his comeback in New Hampshire. David W. Moore wrote (1987, pp. 116, 123):

> In the 1980 primary campaign, the *Union Leader* provided an immense amount of information about the candidates, especially a great deal of negative information about one candidate [Bush] and positive information about the other [Reagan]. If ever a news source can influence voters' opinions, the *Union Leader* should have influenced voters during that campaign. And it did. . . .
>
> On average, readers of the *Union Leader* were more likely than nonreaders to support Ronald Reagan by a margin of 35 to 40 points, a pattern that held true whatever a voter's ideological predisposition (from strong conservative to liberal). Indeed, a simultaneous comparison of numerous factors demonstrates that the *Union Leader* was overwhelmingly the most important influence on the choice Republicans made in the primary election.

Whatever the overall influence of the *Union Leader*, New Hampshire's major news outlet, that influence is at its maximum in addressing Republican primary voters. Reagan campaigned energetically, and ambushed Bush at a key New Hampshire debate by "spontaneously" agreeing to let also-rans onto the platform. It also helped Reagan enormously that the gap between Iowa and New Hampshire was a full month (January 21 to February 26), thus permitting *Union Leader* publicity to counteract Iowa momentum. In 1976, that gap had helped Carter, a "winner" in Iowa; in 1980, it helped Reagan, a "loser."

By the 1980 election the strong interdependence between early delegate selection and media publicity could easily be observed. The "pecking order" of which Germond and Witcover wrote was, after all, a fabrication chiefly valuable in the construction of coherent news stories. The success of Jimmy Carter in 1976, and even more striking, the failure of Henry Jackson, suggested that it would be hard, perhaps impossible, to ascertain the preferences of primary electorates unmediated by the news—and news media evaluations—of how the various candidates were doing. And these characterizations could easily take on the coloration of self-fulfilling prophecies.

1984. Nothing doing on the Republican side; Reagan's incumbency meant no contest in Iowa. Democratic rules were rewritten ostensibly to counteract media influence: states were required to select delegates within a 3-month "window" so that many states would act on any given Tuesday, thus (it was hoped) confounding media attempts to start a single unified bandwagon. The effort was a failure, in part because both Iowa and New Hampshire received exemptions from the window, and continued to act first. On the Democratic side, Walter Mondale overwhelmed everybody, collecting 44.5 percent of the vote in a large field of contenders. Gary Hart came in second with a dismal 14.8 percent of the vote.

This was enough to identify Hart, rather than John Glenn, who finished in 6th place with 5.3 percent of the vote, as the strongest non-Mondale candidate. The news media constructed a horse race out of the unpromising material of the Hart candidacy, gave him extraordinary news coverage for the ensuing week, and boosted him into a win in the New Hampshire primary (Polsby, 1985).[11]

It seems clear enough why the news media need a horse race, given their extraordinary investment in delegate selection coverage and the logic of their competition for business. Iowa caucuses help the news media sort out the story: it was the Iowa caucuses in 1984 that decreed that Gary Hart and not John Glenn should be the "unexpected" horse to make the race against Mondale, and it was the media that made the horse race.

In 1988, with only one week separating Iowa and New Hampshire, the two events might have been expected to interact strongly. Governor Michael Dukakis entered Iowa as the Democratic candidate with the most money and the best organization in the most states—but not in Iowa—and with extremely high and favorable name recognition in New Hampshire, whose Democratic votes are mostly located on the fringes of the Boston metropolitan area. This meant that the only chance the other candidates had to neutralize the favorable impact that the New Hampshire primary was bound to have on the fortunes of the Governor of Massachusetts was in Iowa (Kaus, et al., 1987a; Berke, 1987; Edsall and Broder, 1987; Kaus, et al., 1987b; Schwartz, 1987; Ifill, 1987).

In the event, the Iowa Democratic result did not help the winner there in New Hampshire, mainly because what happened on the Republican side in Iowa had such a strong impact on the Democratic race. As we all know, the big story of Iowa 1988—and there always has to be one big story—was that Pat Robertson came in second and George Bush came in third in the Republican straw poll. And that is how the story played in the news media for the week between Iowa and New Hampshire. Obviously, that was bound to have some impact on the

Republican race—but not as much as on the race on the Democratic side. Because the Robertson blip absorbed so much attention it spoiled the chances of the Democratic winner, Richard Gephardt to capitalize on his Iowa win to become the focal alternative to Michael Dukakis in New Hampshire.

In 1984 Gary Hart was able to parlay a 15 percent second place showing into a media spin that made him the winner in New Hampshire, as figures on late-deciding Democrats showed (Polsby, 1985). In 1976, Jimmy Carter was able to pull out in front of the pack with 29 percent of the vote in the Iowa caucuses. In 1988, a 31 percent win was not enough for Gephardt to turn the same trick. Indeed, the *Wall Street Journal* reported that in the week between the Iowa caucuses and the New Hampshire primary the coverage Gephardt got on the network evening news programs actually diminished from the week before—from 6:05 minutes to 4:55 minutes (Langley, 1988). Thus it is not far-fetched to argue that although the winner in Iowa did not win the nomination of either party, Iowa did in fact play an influential role in determining the 1988 outcome.

What do these historical vignettes teach?

1. Candidates ignore Iowa at their peril. This does not mean that doing badly in Iowa is sufficient to lose everything, or that doing well is sufficient to win everything. It does mean that Iowa can be a tremendous help or a tremendous hindrance to each and every candidacy.
2. This is so not because of Iowa's size but because of its temporal primacy: Iowa results, plus media spin, structure the alternatives for the New Hampshire primary. These two events together plus media spin structure alternatives for everything that follows.

Doing well *in* Iowa takes organization as well as good publicity, because organizations get people to caucuses and sustain their loyalty as the public shufflings and reshufflings take place especially at the Democratic caucuses themselves. Doing well as the *result* of Iowa, however, chiefly requires good publicity; spin control so as to minimize adverse expectations at a minimum, but also, if possible, the good luck to be the story that the national news media converge upon coming out of Iowa and as the first primary approaches. The closer the next event in time, the narrower the temporal gap between Iowa and New Hampshire, the greater the potential that both events can be interpreted together, and thus the more influential the news media response to Iowa overall in the election year.

The translation of these conclusions into grist for the mills of formal theorists of the political process seems straightforward enough. The sequence of Iowa–New Hampshire and so on can be interpreted as reflecting agenda control, goal displacement, or path dependency depending on the theorist's taste in metaphorical language. All these theories recognize the significance of early decisions in determining the options available when it is time to make later ones.

Sequential moves in an organized system may imply adaptation to anticipated choice in the sense of progression toward a specified goal, e.g. the nomination of a presidential candidate. These moves also may imply path dependency or goal displacement or adaptation to experience or historical influence in that alternatives that are possible later in the sequence are constrained by choices that have been made earlier (March, 1988, pp. 2–3, 8–12). It is the palpable importance of the latter sorts of influence in the presidential nominating process that prompts interest in the Iowa caucuses.

Notes

I thank Steven Stehr for superb assistance in pulling a great deal of factual material on Iowa out of the woodwork.

1. See *Presidential Campaign Hotline,* January 4, 1988, pp. 15–16.
2. See *Congressional Quarterly Weekly Report,* August 6, 1988, p. 2161.
3. *Presidential Campaign Hotline,* January 5, 1988, pp. 16–17.
4. Indeed, Henry Brady and Richard Johnston (1987) argue that the main educational effect of the entire primary process for voters is to inform them about candidate viability.
5. See Polsby (1983) for the full argument to this effect, and, for copious evidence, Shafer (1983).
6. In 1976 the Iowa caucuses were held on January 19; in 1980 on January 21; in 1984 on February 20.
7. A number of essays on the progress of the Democratic nomination during 1972 are reprinted in Nelson W. Polsby (1974, pp. 15–51).
8. As Muskie told Theodore White (1973, pp. 81–82), "That previous week . . . I'd been down to Florida, then I flew to Idaho, then I flew to California, then I flew back to Washington to vote in the Senate, and I flew back to California, and then I flew into Manchester and I was hit with this 'Canuck' story. I'm tough physically, but no one could do that. . . ."
9. Elizabeth Drew (1977, pp. 143–144, 466–467) writes of Carter, "Early successes and surprises were big elements in Carter's plan. . . . The basic idea was to show early that the Southerner could do well in the North and could best Wallace in the South. . . . He visited a hundred and fourteen towns in Iowa, beginning in 1975 (and his family made countless other visits). . . ." See also Jules Witcover (1977, p. 114).

10. This was not the first time in 1976 that Apple had puffed Carter. Elizabeth Drew's diary of January 27, 1976 (1977, p. 6), reported, "A story by R.W. Apple, Jr. in the *Times* last October saying that Carter was doing well in Iowa was itself a political event, prompting other newspaper stories that Carter was doing well in Iowa, and then more news magazine and television coverage for Carter than might otherwise have been his share."

11. In the eight day gap between Iowa and New Hampshire, Gary Hart went from 10 per cent in the public opinion polls to a 41 per cent vote in the New Hampshire primary itself. See Peter Hart's comments in the *Presidential Campaign Hotline*, January 25, 1988, p. 19.

References

Adams, William C. 1987. 'As New Hampshire Goes.' In Gary R. Orren and Nelson W. Polsby, eds., *Media and Momentum*. Chatham, NJ: Chatham House.

Apple, R. W., Jr. January 20, 1976. Carter Defeats Bayh By 2–1 in Iowa Vote. *New York Times*.

———. January 25, 1988. Iowa's Weighty Caucuses: Significance By Accident. *New York Times*.

Berke, Richard. September 6, 1987. Iowa Eclipsing New Hampshire Among Hopefuls. *New York Times*.

Brady, Henry E., and Richard Johnston. 1987. What's the Primary Message: Horse Race or Issue Journalism? In Gary R. Orren and Nelson W. Polsby, eds., *Media and Momentum*. Chatham, NJ: Chatham House.

Drew, Elizabeth. 1977. *American Journal: The Events of 1976*. New York: Random House.

Edsall, Thomas B., and David S. Broder. October 3, 1987. Dukakis' New Hampshire Campaign Not Unraveled by Biden Videotape. *Washington Post*.

Germond, Jack and Jules Witcover. 1981. *Blue Smoke and Mirrors*. New York: Viking.

Ifill, Gwen. November 20, 1987. Bush and Dukakis Far Ahead in Poll. *Washington Post*.

Kaus, Mickey, et al. July 20, 1987. Yes We Have a Front-Runner. *Newsweek*.

———. October 12, 1987. Now, a Dukakis Fiasco. *Newsweek*.

Langley, Monica. February 16, 1988. In Pre-New Hampshire Flurry, Images Prevail, and TV Coverage May be Pivotal to Candidates. *Wall Street Journal*.

March, James G. 1988. *Decisions and Organizations*. Oxford, England: Basil Blackwell.

May, Ernest R., and Janet Fraser, eds., 1973. *Campaign '72: The Managers Speak*. Cambridge: Harvard University Press.

Moore, David W. 1987. The *Manchester Union Leaders* in the New Hampshire Primary. In Gary R. Orren and Nelson W. Polsby, eds., *Media and Momentum*. Chatham, NJ: Chatham House.

Muskie Campaign: Cautious Pace By the Man in Front. April 16, 1971. *Congressional Quarterly Weekly Report*. p. 857.

Polsby, Nelson W. 1974. *Political Promises: Essays and Commentary on American Politics* New York: Oxford.

_____. 1981. The Democratic Nomination. In Austin Ranney, ed., *The American Elections of 1980* Washington, DC: AEI.

_____. 1983. *Consequences of Party Reform.* New York: Oxford.

_____. 1985. The Democratic Nomination and the Evolution of the Party System. In Austin Ranney, ed., *The American Elections of 1984.* Durham, NC: Duke University Press.

Schram, Martin. 1977. *Running For President 1976.* New York: Stein and Day.

Schwartz, Maralee. November 11, 1987. Dukakis Still a Top Fund-Raiser. *Washington Post.*

Shafer, Byron E. 1983. *Quiet Revolution: The Struggle for the Democratic Party and the Shaping of Post-Reform Politics.* New York: Russell Sage.

Witcover, Jules. 1977. *Marathon: The Pursuit of the Presidency 1972-1976.* New York: Viking.

7

Who Is Vulnerable to the Iowa Caucuses?

Raymond E. Wolfinger

We have persuasive evidence that, contrary to the common journalistic assumption, the state of Iowa is not so unrepresentative a place for the first major authoritative expressions of candidate preference. Of course, it's one thing to talk about the state of Iowa's representativeness and another to talk about the representativeness of Iowa caucus' participants. The evidence that people who attend Iowa caucuses are a fairly representative bunch may reflect in part their wider range of choices: the whole candidate lineup is here, before being winnowed by the caucuses. With the maximum range of contenders from right to left and top to bottom, one might think that some kinds of people—those who are particularly attracted to one or another kind of candidate who is likely to be winnowed out—may be more likely to participate in Iowa than in other states.

As against this guess, there is evidence that most individuals' candidate preferences are fairly soft in the early part of the season and progressively harden as the choices narrow and as voters learn more about the candidates. To put it another way, we know from Larry Bartels that the importance of momentum is greatest in the first part of the primary season and declines as the spring wears on, as potential primary voters learn more and more about the dwindling number of choices available to them. This suggests that early in the season the followers of most candidates include a sprinkling of well-informed enthusiasts and probably a larger number of not-so-well-informed chasers after fashion, bandwagon riders, and the like. This may not be equally true of all candidates, however. I will return to this point below.

Reminiscing about the importance of the Iowa caucuses often leads to quotations of R.W. Apple's front page *New York Times* report on the outcome in Iowa in 1976. Apple is said to have made Jimmy Carter the front runner, thus producing the enormous leap in visibility that led to his showing in New Hampshire and thence to the White House. In this view, Apple's story joins *Uncle Tom's Cabin* and a handful of other literary pieces that changed history. This gives him too much credit. I doubt that Mr. Apple was out of step with his colleagues in the print and electronic media. For example, morning network interview shows featured Jimmy Carter the day after the Iowa caucuses (he had thoughtfully gone to New York from Iowa).

"Contest" is the common synonym for "election." The most salient thing about a contest usually is the identity of the winner, and upsets are always particularly newsworthy. Journalists generally are not in business to unearth complications. It is neither shameful nor surprising that journalists of all sorts concluded that the lead story from Iowa in 1976 was the identity of the candidate who had received the greatest amount of support. The fact that he was a hitherto unknown one-term southern governor made the story all the better. Apple deserves neither singular praise nor blame; his story captured what his colleagues were saying about the outcome. If one candidate is a sure winner, then the story is the identity of the second-place finisher, hence all the attention to Gary Hart after the Iowa caucuses four years ago.

These remarks are preliminary to consideration of the most interesting thing about the Iowa caucuses: their winnowing of the field of candidates. We can all understand that an important function of the early events is to reduce the number of candidates. While the outcome of the Iowa caucuses will not anticipate either party's eventual nomination, those same results will certainly produce fairly convincing evidence that some candidates are no longer in the race. Iowa is not so much a king-maker as a peasant-maker.

It would be a substantial mistake to attribute this particular consequence of the Iowa caucuses to the Democratic party reforms of the 1970s, events that are so frequently blamed for the salient features of the nomination process we study. The best evidence for this is pre-reform primaries that were pretty effective peasant-makers. We could begin with the 1948 Republican primary in Oregon, which removed Harold Stassen as a contender for his party's nomination. At the time, journalistic commentary attributed Stassen's defeat to his humiliation by Thomas E. Dewey in a debate about outlawing the Communist party.

In 1960, the Democratic primary in Wisconsin had the effect of eliminating Hubert Humphrey as a realistic contender. Humphrey was, in any event, a longshot. When it turned out that he could not win convincingly in a state that not only adjoined Minnesota, but in many respects was a political carbon copy, party leaders concluded that he was unlikely to lead them to victory in November. The distinction between kingmaking and peasant making is illustrated by the fact that John F. Kennedy could hardly be said to have clinched his nomination by his victory in Wisconsin. The reason was Kennedy's religion; while he did well in Wisconsin, he ran a great deal worse in protestant than catholic areas, thereby failing to dispel fears that his religion would be a fatal handicap in the fall. In 1968, unimpressive performances in New Hampshire and Wisconsin put Lyndon Johnson out of the race and Eugene McCarthy and Robert Kennedy into it. Whatever the merit of recent stories that Johnson intended all along not to run in 1968, it is certainly the case that these early primaries were the occasion for his withdrawal.

In those pre-reform days, party politicians were the relevant audience for primary outcomes, the ones who decided that the performance of various contenders raised or lowered their chances of getting the nomination, if only because of the clues they provided about general election appeal. Now the situation is more complex. The press surely is party of the current critical audience. We all know about the famous game of "expectations," how the press concluded, for example, that Edmund Muskie had not won the 1972 New Hampshire primary by a large enough margin. Or, for that matter, that Lyndon Johnson, winner as a write-in candidate in New Hampshire in 1968, nevertheless had not met expectations.

Another part of the audience is potential campaign contributors who may decide, watching the failure of a possible favorite, that they will not throw their good money after somebody else's bad. We know from the research of Larry Bartels that members of the mass public also attend to the outcome of primaries; they are the main audience for momentum.

We can begin to understand the winnowing function by looking at the exceptions, contenders whose candidacies were not destroyed by one or even a series of defeats. One example can be found in the 1952 Republican nomination fight, when Robert Taft and Dwight Eisenhower exchanged a series of blows that would have put many a contender out of the race. The fight went down to the wire with neither man knocked out by losing, until the convention chose Eisenhower. The same was true in 1976, when a string of defeats at the hands of a incumbent Republican president were not sufficient to drive Ronald Reagan out. Beginning with his surprise victory in North Carolina, Reagan came right back and slugged it out with President Gerald Ford until the eve of the convention. Perhaps winnowing down to two candidates for a nomination is accomplished more readily than winnowing down to one.

With regard to the audience for the winnowing function, we should remember that in 1976 the nomination of Jimmy Carter was sealed by the announcement of Mayor Richard Daley that Carter had sewed up the nomination. It might be considered an irony that Carter, the ultimate outsider, was crowned by Daley, widely considered the prince of darkness by reformers.

Another way to ask the same question might be, why do some people become peasants faster than others? Or, when is the California primary important? A persistent if not often salient grievance among politically-interested Californians is the fairly common irrelevance of that state in the primary season because the nominees are known long before its early June primary date. But this poormouthing overlooks the fact that every once in a while the choices are not known so soon, and then California's primary, far from being an irrelevant afterthought, is the decisive event. This was certainly the case for the Republicans in 1964, when Barry Goldwater sealed his nomination by defeating Nelson Rockefeller on the last day of the season. The same was true in 1968 when Robert Kennedy appeared on his way to the nomination for a few short minutes before his assassination on the night of his victory over Eugene McCarthy.

Just why does a primary defeat knock a candidate out of the race? One reason certainly is that candidates need contributions and potential donors are discouraged by the prospect that they will be wasting their money. This means, then, that a candidate who already has a huge treasure chest can more easily sustain the loss of one or two early contests because he will be able to sustain himself on his stored-up fat, until he gets to a state or states where he can do better. In the 1988 campaign, the obvious example of this proposition was Vice President Bush, who was so well-financed that he could easily conduct campaigns in New Hampshire and Super Tuesday after he lost in Iowa. In other words, the peasant-making process operates when a candidate can no longer pay for his campaign.

Some candidates are in the race on spec, hoping that they will catch on. If they don't demonstrate sufficient appeal to indifferent but potentially interested voters, they will never experience the rise in the polls enjoyed by examples of this phenomenon such as Jimmy Carter and George McGovern. Bruce Babbitt and Pierre du Pont are contemporary examples of candidates running on spec.

Candidates who have an identifiable and relatively enthusiastic con-stituency are a good deal more immune to the winnowing process than are contenders who lack such backing. In 1976, Gerald Ford's early victories failed to put Ronald Reagan out of the race because Reagan had such a constituency: true believer right-wing Republicans who were dissatisfied with Ford's compromising and negotiating, preferred real red meat, and therefore found Reagan more to their liking. Much the same could be said of 1952, when the liberal wing of the Republican party was a good deal stronger and more self-confident, and therefore unlikely to be easily discouraged when Eisenhower suffered early defeats. And Taft, of course, appealed to the Main street heart of the party.

It seems to me that in 1988 only one candidate for sure and perhaps a second candidate had this kind of support. The certainty is, of course, Jesse Jackson. As his strength in the latter weeks of the 1984 campaign demonstrated, Jackson has the support of almost all black Democrats. Losses in 1984 did not deter his supporters nor dampen their enthusiasm. Indeed, Jackson gained strength among blacks as the weeks wore on. It is not surprising that Jackson was in the 1988 campaign throughout. He has a constituency, the people in that constituency know who they are and know who Jackson is and know why they support him, and none of that was likely to change if Jackson lost in Iowa, and in New Hampshire, and in many states thereafter.

The possible second member of this select group is Pat Robertson. He seemed to be able to elicit a good deal of enthusiasm in certain quarters, from white evangelical, fundamentalist protestants. There is no question that there are substantial numbers of these people and that they are enthusiastic about their cause, and seem committed to Robertson as their leader. Most Jackson supporters are easily identifiable, but this is not the case for Robertson backers, since the dimensions of the movement that he represents are unclear. If it had turned out that he and he alone could have appealed to these people, then he might well have been in the race a long time despite his inability to win. We might speculate that candidates like Jackson and Robertson have at least two other things in common: they are likely to do better in caucuses than primaries because their supporters are much more intense and less numerous than the backers of other contenders; and those supporters probably have been in their corners for a fairly long time.

The contenders for the nomination in 1988 did not seem a terribly imposing lot; one might have imagined that no commanding figure would emerge on either side sufficiently soon to capture a majority of the convention delegates. The event that has been anticipated with greater or lesser degrees of enthusiasm for some years might have occurred; a convention with no clear front runner.

If and when this happens, the delegates will become a good deal more important actors than they have been in the past. Up until now, whether before or after reform, the delegates have been rather like those human chess pieces that French kings are said to have used for their amusement at Versailles. Instead of being merely symbols of numbers of votes, the delegates will become sentient beings who make decisions themselves. If this happens, who these delegates are will be a good deal more important than it is now. Doubtless we will want to spend more time finding out what kind of people they are and how they put themselves forward, and how well their candidates know them before they're chosen.

People who deplore the current nominating system often do so because they think the process chooses candidates on the basis of their appeal to a fairly narrow band of caucus goers and primary voters in their own parties. The result, so it is said, is nominees who may be very good at stirring up the activists at one or the other end of the spectrum, but not so good at appealing to the broad middle ground where elections are won. This result has been contrasted with the old days, when the party leaders picked somebody on the basis of his likely appeal to a majority of voters. Perhaps, but in thinking about the past we should remember that judgments of who can win are often fairly ideologically based, and that the interest of party leaders in any particular place was not identifying the prime nationwide candidate, but rather finding someone to lead the ticket with maximum effect in their own city, county, or state. Somebody who can make the strongest appeal in any particular place need not be the one who can do best across the country. As I think about the most appealing leader of the ticket in my home town of Berkeley, for example, I find it hard to believe that such a person would have a similar effect in many places except perhaps Cambridge, Ann Arbor, and Madison.

In other words, the disinterested leaders whose peer review provided nominees like Warren G. Harding and John W. Davis may have been pursuing interests no less parochial than the whale savers and abortion fighters who are said to be so disproportionately influential in the contemporary nominating process.

Notes

Many helpful comments were made on an earlier draft of this piece by Michael G. Hagen, Nelson W. Polsby, Austin Ranney, Peverill Squire, and Barbara Kaye Wolfinger.

8

Democracy, Media, and Presidential Primaries

Christopher H. Achen

Introduction

Americans want many things from their presidential selection system, including both stable policies and quick democratic response, distinct policy choices and moderate parties, exciting entertainment and no real risks. From the candidates, they look for good moral character ·and political muscle, idealism and pragmatic virtues, personal appeal and insider skills, a fresh face and a respected name, new ideas and familiar values. And, sometimes almost as an afterthought, they want a wise and capable president inaugurated in January.

Most presidents prove disappointing. Here as elsewhere, Americans have been mystified when they failed to satisfy all their political wishes simultaneously. From time to time, they have sought institutional remedies in reform of the presidential selection system.

The history of the last two decades of party reform will be familiar to most readers. In 1968, the Democrats nominated Vice President and former Minnesota Senator Hubert Humphrey. Humphrey was a brilliant politician who had given years of service to the party, but his views on the Vietnam War were sufficiently unpopular that he was represented in primary states only by favorite-son surrogates, and they were beaten badly almost everywhere. Humphrey got the nomination by winning the convention states, where party professionals dominated the delegate choice.

After the debacle of the Chicago convention and the narrow loss in November to Richard Nixon, the Democratic party altered its internal rules to give more weight to the middle class, black, and other amateur activists who had displaced the party professionals and big-city bosses in control of the party's voter base. For many of the reformers, the goal

169

170   *Christopher H. Achen*

of the reforms was to make impossible the future nomination of another candidates like Humphrey. The means chosen was to make the party more "representative" of its supporters. Combined with subsequent reforms by the Republicans and a shift to primaries by many states, the result was a far more "democratic" system, in the sense that a much larger number of citizens played a role in nominations than before.

Throughout this process, relatively little attention was paid to the profound disagreements within the theory of "democracy." Virtually everyone professed to want more of it, not just in the unexceptionable sense of giving all parts of population equal access to the process, but also of substituting plebiscitary mechanisms for the judgment of professional party members. So honorific was the term "democracy" that critics of the reforms were reduced to arguing that primaries were themselves not very democratic. As Squire notes in his contribution to this volume, Iowa itself has not escaped criticism on this score.

Alternative Theories of Democracy

Much of the reform movement in the Democratic Party has proceeded on the implicit assumption that the more representative the electorate was of the adult populace, the better the decisions were likely to be. For those who accept this framework, the current presidential selection process can be evaluated by asking how well the composition of the primary and caucus electorates matches the voting age population. Several excellent studies have been carried out along these lines, notably Ranney (1972) and Lengle (1981). The paper in this volume by Stone, Abramowitz and Rapoport is another attractive example of the genre, and it constitutes the best information we have about Iowa caucus-goers.

Stone and his colleagues demonstrate that Iowa caucuses are disproportionately attended by older, richer, better educated citizens, and perhaps more importantly, that they tend to come from the ideological wings of their parties. They also show that Michigan and Virginia caucus-attenders are even less representative of their populations. Some have used data like these to argue that the present system is not really very democratic at all, and thus that it has no special advantage over state nominating conventions controlled by party professionals.

This argument is implicitly comparative, and all comparisons are relative. Thus Hagen's chapter asks not whether primary electorates are unrepresentative in an absolute sense, but whether they are worse than general electorates. Using the very large national sample from the 1976 Current Population Survey, he finds that presidential primary electorates are quite representative of the registered population, and not much less representative than American general electorates. Due to the limits of

Census Bureau questionnaires, Hagen confines himself to demographic comparisons. This leaves open the question of ideological representativeness underscored by Stone, Abramowitz and Rapoport. But Hagen's work does raise the possibility that, if we decide to restrict the primary system for lack of representative electorates, we might have to cut back on general elections as well.

So drastic a conclusion raises issues best answered by an appeal to first principles. Is greater representativeness always desirable? Is its importance mostly symbolic, or do we expect better representation to yield better choices?

As is well known, the great apostle of democracy, Rousseau (1947), distinguished two outcomes toward which the democratic process might tend. The first, and more desirable, was the "general will." Although Rousseau was never very clear about its meaning, the term connoted correct social judgment or the "common good," a concept that derived from medieval political thought. For the practical purposes of judging electoral systems, we might be inclined to identify it with long-term historical judgment, e.g., the election of Lincoln was a better choice than the election of Grant.

How might the general will be ascertained at the time of the election? In an ideal society, Rousseau believed, majority rule of all citizens tended to produce the general will. "Each citizen, in giving his suffrage, states his mind on that question; and the general will is found by counting the votes" (Rousseau, 1947, pp. 95–96). Here, then, is a theoretical mechanism that connects representativeness and good decisions. In Rousseau's ideal world, more democracy and more representativeness could only be beneficial.

Even for Rousseau, however, majority rule was no panacea. The presence of groups or factions might generate instead "the will of all," a vector sum of self-interested pressures with no teleological properties whatever:

> There is frequently much difference between the will of all and the general will. The latter regards only the common interest; the former regards private interest, and is indeed but a sum of private wills: but remove from these same wills the pluses and minuses that cancel each other, and then the general will remains as the sum of the differences.
>
> If, when the people, sufficiently informed, deliberated, there was to be no communication among them, from the grand total of trifling differences the general will would always result, and their resolutions be always good. But when cabals and associations are formed at the expense of the great association, the will of each such association, though general with regard to its members, is private with regard to the State: it can then be said

no longer that there are as many voters as men, but only as many as there are associations. By this means the differences being less numerous, they produce a result less general.

Thus when a few groups dominate, democracy has no great attraction. Rousseau himself favored aristocracy or monarchy when the general will was not likely to proceed from majority rule. Only when the distortions of group process could be avoided was democracy desirable.

The irony of much contemporary thinking about American politics has been its simultaneous aversion to Rousseau's medievalisms and attachment to the conclusions that depend upon them. Abandoning the effort to define the common good, Bentley (1908), Truman (1971) and others described American government as "group process," the push and pull of self interested factions. At most, the common welfare might be represented by "rules of the game" partisans (Truman, 1971, ch. 16), but that group was likely to be latent much of the time and more concerned with process than with substance. In any case it had no privileged status.

This description of group politics extends to the electoral process (Truman, 1971, ch. 10). In contemporary presidential primaries in particular, the number of major factions within a particular state's primary electorate might be rather small—just the more ideological activists and their opponents, for example. In short, presidential selection in America is widely viewed as operating under just those conditions for which Rousseau thought democracy unsuited.

Yet while Rousseau's logic is scorned, his conclusions about an ideal society are widely applied to the American primary system. Where democratization is concerned, Americans believe, the more the merrier. Civics classes preach the representativeness of American elections as if that quality were self justifying. Rational-choice modelers in the Downsian tradition seek electoral equilibria in which voter preferences are taken as given, and the possibility that one might want to modify, educate, or restrain them is nearly always ignored. And both parties are reformed under the banner of "more democracy."

All this is quite alien to the spirit of *The Federalist Papers*. The plebiscitary theory of democracy has never had much appeal in American political thought or the political science profession. And even those Americans of a more radical democratic temperament have long since given up on the notion that democracy tends to the general will. (Indeed, Arrow [1963] has shown that just making sense of the will of all involves profound difficulties.)

Nor has some other widely acceptable argument replaced Rousseau's: We have lost what little faith we ever had as a society in the connection between more democracy and better decisions. Thus as an intellectual proposition, our uncritical collective enthusiasm for further political democratization is rather mysterious.[1]

The kind of democratic theory that has long enjoyed a special attraction for students of American politics is the doctrine of responsible party government (Ranney, 1954). In its various incarnations, this version of democratic thinking abhors representative primary electorates. Party government models of democracy are designed for a world of interest group pressures (e.g., Schattschneider, 1942; Truman, 1971, ch. 16). Their holy grail is not representativeness, as in the plebiscite, but rather programatically coherent parties strong enough to fend off the narrow self-interests and overcome the numerous veto points of the American governmental system.

In the case of the European socialist parties, from which much American thinking on strong parties derives, the choice of party candidates is deliberately insulated from the electorate as a whole. Choice is restricted to party members and elites, a small fraction of the population more engaged in politics than the average citizen, more strongly identified with the party, and more extreme ideologically (e.g., Beer, 1965, pp. 79–91). In short, precisely those characteristics of primary electorates which have been condemned in recent years have been celebrated in the main tradition of American political science as the key to popular sovereignty.

It goes without saying that a caucus in an Iowa grade school is distinguishable from the local meeting of a British Labour constituency party meeting. One may think well of the latter without endorsing the former, and vice-versa. The point is rather that representativeness or its absence has rarely been taken as the central issue in contemporary democratic theory of mass industrial democracies. Indeed, for Schumpeter (1947), it was strictly irrelevant: he wanted the parties to choose candidates on their own, with the voters participating only at the general election and making their selection solely on the basis of competence to govern.

For most democratic theory, of course, representativeness is not irrelevant. Turnout matters. However, it pales before the question of where political power is to be located. And the structure of interest groups, unions, mass movements, and political parties will always have more effect on the distribution of power than does turnout.

For the literature on the representativeness of presidential primary electorates, then, an important issue for the next round of research is this: Which theory of democracy is under discussion? If plebiscitary government is unappealing, then why is unrepresentativeness bad? In particular, if primary electorates are more ideologically coherent and distinct from the other party than mass electorates, might that not be a contribution toward more effective government?

Answering these questions is impossible without a firm factual understanding of who participates in primaries and caucuses, and Stone and his colleagues and Hagen in this volume have ably contributed to that goal. But we will need additional conceptual advances as well. Until our collective theoretical understanding is clearer, we will lack the ability to speak with confidence about the value of democratizing the American presidential selection process.

The Role of the Media

The daunting conceptual tangles of normative and empirical democratic theory have led many analysts to adopt a simpler and more pragmatic criterion for evaluating presidential selection. In this approach, the precise mechanisms at work are slighted in favor of a focus on outcomes. The change in party rules creates a quasi-experiment, and the calibre of presidential nominees and near-nominees before and after is compared. On the Democratic side, George McGovern, Jimmy Carter, Gary Hart, and Ronald Reagan are said to demonstrate the weakness of the present system relative to what came before them.

Particular attention is paid to the role of the media. Especially in cases like Carter and Hart, it is said, the media created a powerful candidacy from accidents of the early primary season. Carter won Iowa narrowly in 1976; Hart was a distant second (nearly third) eight years later. Each parlayed his showing into intense media coverage and a major candidacy. And in both cases, the argument goes, subsequent events have demonstrated that neither should have been president.

Arguments of this kind enjoy a certain persuasiveness; they also have their dangers. The same system that gave us Reagan, McGovern, Carter, and nearly Hart also produced consummate Washington insiders Gerald Ford, Walter Mondale, and George Bush. Is this record better or worse than the system that produced James Davis, Warren Harding, Calvin Coolidge, Al Smith, Herbert Hoover, and Franklin Delano Roosevelt? As soon as the question is put this way, the complexities of historical judgment, the dispersion in small samples, and the distortions of contemporary perspective become painfully apparent.

An example may help make the point clear. As of 1981, no president elected in almost thirty years had served two full terms. In the early 1980s, it became a cliche in political science that structural features of American political life had so weakened the office that the second term had become almost unattainable. At that point, looking back over the last few candidates and elections, the case looked strong. Combined with the long standing superstition that presidents elected in years divisible by twenty fail to live out their terms, Reagan's prospects appeared dismal indeed. But of course, these expectations were followed immediately by the strong Reagan presidency and successful incumbent candidacy in 1984.

My point here is that the evidence supporting these forecasts was of approximately the same quantity and quality as our judgments on the candidates produced by the new presidential selection system. Any small set of case studies must be studied carefully and skeptically, not because they contain no wisdom, but because we are so susceptible to misjudging what their wisdom is. And in the absence of a strong theoretical understanding of so complex a system as the presidential nominating process, misjudgments are almost inevitable. One recalls Bagehot's (1966, p. 81) verdict on the American presidential process that "the notion of employing a man of unknown smallness at a crisis of unknown greatness is to our minds simply ludicrous." He was referring to Lincoln.[2]

Thoughts of this sort keep me from an unqualified endorsement of the strongly argued and delightfully written work by Nelson Polsby and Richard Fenno. Both make the case for media influence, Polsby in his overview chapter on recent contests, Fenno (1988) in an intensive study of the John Glenn candidacy in 1984. "The news media" Polsby writes, "constructed a horse race out of the unpromising material of the Hart candidacy, gave him extraordinary news coverage for the ensuing week, and boosted him into a win in the New Hampshire primary." Fenno summarizes his findings by saying:

> By setting their expectations for him too high and by pressuring his advisors to agree, the media had set John Glenn up for the kill. . . . Further, by making Glenn's failure THE story, they effectively took him out of the race. . . . Unwilling to downgrade his standing when they could have done so several weeks earlier, they propped him up so that they could write him off after Iowa.

Persuasive as these two accounts are, they are not the only possible interpretations of the events they describe. Fenno himself mentions a few pages later that Glenn's subsequent collapse in the New Hampshire polls may have been due to something other than the media's set-up job. He quotes a New Hampshire pollster as saying that Glenn's sixth-place finish with 5 percent of the vote in Iowa destroyed Glenn's own key argument for his candidacy, namely that he was the most electable Democrat. If so, the Glenn collapse would be just what we would expect in a world of neutral media reports, no media prop ups, no media-induced momentum, and sensible, reasonably well informed voters.

Similar remarks apply to the Hart candidacy. As Bartels shows, many Democratic voters were looking for an alternative to Mondale in 1984, but few had found one before Iowa. Every Democratic presidential season since 1968 has featured a lunch bucket candidate against a wine-and-cheese candidate, but before the primaries in 1984, only one side had an obvious standardbearer. Then in Iowa, Mondale won easily, but the unknown Hart was second with 15 percent of the vote, defeating well known figures such as McGovern and Glenn. After a week of intense media coverage, Hart went on to win New Hampshire and a series of other states before finally falling just short at the convention.

Like the Glenn campaign, the Hart near-success is subject to a variety of interpretations. Suppose, for example, that after Iowa millions of anti-Mondale voters reasoned that while well known candidates McGovern and Glenn were obviously near the limits of what they could accomplish, Hart had the potential for great improvement. He was a Senator, he was young and attractive, no scandals were attached to him (yet), he was from the middle class, anti-Mondale wing of the party, and he had done well with few resources and no name recognition. In short, Hart was the right kind of Democrat for an anti-Mondale voter, and he was electorally credible. Nearly half the country's Democrats jumped to him after Iowa, in much the same way that the party leaders leapt on the John Kennedy bandwagon in those pre-reform, pre-mass primary, pre-momentum days of 1960 when he proved he could win a Protestant state primary like West Virginia.

This version of the Hart story downplays the "accident" of his being second rather than third by a few percentage points in Iowa. Mondale had proved he was a major candidate; everyone else but Hart had proved he was not. Given his name recognition and resources, Hart had vastly outperformed the rest of the field. Moreover, he was clearly from the anti-Mondale side of the major cleavage in the party, a side that had no one else available.

In my judgment, Hart would have been a major contender whether he finished a few points higher or lower than McGovern, and McGovern would not have been. Hart's take-off after Iowa was deterministic, not stochastic. In that sense, Hart was no fluke created by media expectations, no random event in a lottery, but a smart candidate capturing a large fraction of the electorate looking for someone like him.

For anti-Mondale Democrats after Iowa, the evidence that among those running, Hart was ideologically the right candidate for them in 1984 was overwhelming. They may not have known much about this moral character (no more, say, than was known about the marital fidelity of Franklin Roosevelt or John Kennedy when they died), and the details of his policy views and character traits may have been hazy for awhile

TABLE 8.1   1984 Iowa Democratic Caucus Voters' Evaluations of Candidates

Candidate	Evaluation (Average Utility)
Gary Hart	4.39
Walter Mondale	4.37
George McGovern	3.29
Alan Cranston	2.15
Jesse Jackson	2.06
John Glenn	1.89
John Anderson	1.63

Source: Brady (1988).

in places where no primaries had been held (as the Bartels and Brady articles in this volume demonstrate for national samples), but Hart's position in the party and his electoral appeal could presumably be estimated with some confidence by those who cared to, and people who actually voted in a given week undoubtedly paid more attention than most.

Striking evidence in support of this view has recently been developed by Brady (1988), who is no friend to the hypothesis. Using data collected by Stone and his colleagues, Brady uses sophisticated scaling techniques to derive estimates of how Iowa Democratic caucus attenders evaluated the presidential candidates in 1984. Some voters liked a candidate but failed to vote for him due to low expectations that he could win. Brady is assessing likes and dislikes, not the subsequent downgrading due to poor prospects. Since the poll was taken before the Iowa caucuses, the voters' evaluations reflect pre-media hype, pre-momentum evaluations.

The conventional view argues that Hart finished poorly in Iowa due to small popular appeal, and attributes his subsequent rise to media support after Iowa. On this position, Hart's evaluation by Iowa voters before the caucuses should be low. The alternate view proposed here suggests that he was popular when the voters got a close look at him, but did poorly until his supporters received a clear signal as to how numerous they were and thus how good his electoral chances were. On this position, Hart's evaluation by Iowa voters before the caucuses should be higher than anyone's but Mondale's, and perhaps just as high.

Brady's findings are given in Table 8.1. The data show that Hart and Mondale were evaluated virtually dead-even in Iowa, just as they were over the remainder of the primary season in the other states. In other words, Iowa voters facing no media blitz came to just the same conclusion as everyone else. This is a bizarre anomaly for the conventional view, and it represents a dramatic predictive failure for the view that media create candidates. On the other hand, it is just what one would expect for the alternative position proposed here. Certainly nothing in the sum of evidence before us contradicts an assumption that the electorate responds more to fundamental appeal than to the power of media suggestion.

On this view, "momentum" need not be irrational herd-following. It may be instead a reasonable calculation as to the strongest candidate of one's own persuasion or tendance. Thus I would expect that most voters do not know issue positions and personal styles early on, but that they do know group loyalties and basic political standing. Not where Hart and Mondale differ on import restrictions, but who is closer to the unions. Not whether Cuomo and Gephardt are equally well loved by fellow politicians, but which of the two is the major national figure. And even when voters cannot actually articulate these considerations, they may take them into account implicitly.

Bartels shows that Hart would have done less well without Big Mo, and his calculations are sophisticated and credible. But he does not construe them simplistically, and indeed they support more than one interpretation. Bartels' estimates of Hart-without-momentum in effect deny the voters their option to abandon candidates who cannot win. That is a reasonable definition of momentum, but not necessarily something one wants to prevent. Kennedy would have done a lot less well without beating Humphrey in West Virginia, but we ordinarily interpret that result as party professionals making a better decision after they got more information about Kennedy's appeal. Why should the voters watching Hart not be credited with the same savvy?

On this interpretation, the voters are "rational" in the strong sense that they not only use their information efficiently, but that the amount of it available to them is not too meager for the purposes of a democracy. Perhaps more importantly, there is no need to attribute motives to the media beyond a desire to report primary results accurately. They need not set anyone up nor construct any candidacies. The dramatic ups and downs of the primary season are accounted for, not by the private motives of the media, but by the personal commonsense judgments of the voters having outlandish aggregate effects. To paraphrase Pogo: it's not them, it's us.

This view of the media has strong consequences for evaluating their role in the primaries. For example, contrary to what is sometimes assumed, it would be irresponsible for the media not to give Hart more coverage after Iowa than Mondale. It would also be irresponsible not to cover Iowa and New Hampshire more than the large states later in the race. The voter's need for information is greatest early on, and she needs to learn more about the less familiar face. If the media's goal is simply to inform the voters, then giving media coverage in each state proportional to the number of delegates is irrational by conventional rational decision theory criteria, and more relevantly, irresponsible by the standards of common-sense democratic theory.[3]

This pre-theory of the primaries, if proven correct by further research, would not only alter our evaluations of voters and the media, but it would also make quite different predictions than the current scholarly consensus. If the media need to create a two-person horse race after Iowa, as is often said, then finishing third should be a substantial disadvantage every year. On the other hand, if fundamental appeal is as important as I have claimed, then a candidate ought to be able to run third in Iowa in 1988 in either party, perhaps even a disappointing third with much negative publicity, survive it, gain momentum at some later stage, and be nominated. And they did. The evidence of 1988 seems to provide yet another predictive failure for the view that fundamentals matter less than media-induced momentum.

At this stage of our knowledge, the alternative interpretation I have sketched above remains somewhat speculative. Certainly the conventional interpretation is better supported by intuitive political judgment, and one ought never discount the judgment of on-the-scene observers. Yet the alternative interpretation fits the hard evidence at least as well.

How might these explanatory frameworks be distinguished? At bottom, the two view disagree on how the primary system would work if everyone were reasonable. Was Glenn's demise murder or suicide? Was Hart almost inevitable or a sheer fluke? The answers turn on how gullible the voters are and how biased the media are, and on whether major candidacies can collapse overnight and new faces emerge without someone somewhere behaving unreasonably.

It is perhaps obvious that those who argue for sensible voters and undistorting media will be forced to construct a fully rational model of the system if they wish to truly prove their case. It is perhaps not so obvious that proponents of media distortion and ill-formed voters need such a model as well. For as John Harsanyi (1977, ch. 2) points out, one must understand perfectly-informed rational behavior in a social situation before one can demonstrate that other behavior is ill informed or irrational. Apparently irrational behavior has often been shown to be perfectly sensible given people's choice options and competitive situation. Hence analysts have grown properly cautious about employing irrationality, low information, or ulterior motives as explanations of unattractive social outcomes.

As yet, no complete model of rational behavior in a stylized primary system is available, although major efforts have been made (notably Brady, 1984). Thus we cannot yet meet the Harsanyi criterion for judging the primary process. Our theoretical ignorance permits interpretations of the system in which media and voters are poor democratic citizens and candidate choices are largely arbitrary. It also permits the construction of models in which everyone behaves as an admirably Bayesian decision maker, the people are not hopelessly ignorant, the media have no private agenda, and candidates reflect fundamental ideological fissures within the parties. The data do not yet permit a decisive choice between these two views. Inevitably, then, both sides' judgments about the media and its impact on momentum must be weighed with appropriate scientific caution.

What Is to Be Done?

Our knowledge of the new presidential selection system has advanced remarkably in the last few years. The authors represented in this book are responsible for much of the best work. Yet more remains to be done.

First and centrally, we need a stronger foundation in democratic theory for both formal theoretical work and empirical studies. For example, if we cannot say what the voters should know about a candidate, judgments of their perspicacity will inevitably be driven by our personal assessments of their recent choices. Tying empirical work to the political thinking of Rousseau, Schumpeter and the Webbs will transform debates over "representativeness" and "democracy."

Second and equally critically, more realistic but fully game theoretic models of the primary process are needed. At present, we reason about the social process mostly by analogy to the individual. If a sensible individual would alter her judgments on candidates only slowly and deliberately over the primary season, then surely a rational social judgment would change in the same way. If, on the other hand, candidates can explode into prominence or evanesce overnight, then we are naturally inclined to think that someone, probably the media, is serving socially irrelevant goals and causing the observed distortions.

Unfortunately, as Schelling (1978) and others have long reminded us, no such inference is possible: sensible individual behavior may lead to dramatic, discontinuous social consequences. For all we know, such behavior may be inevitable in any leadership selection process that extends over time, including bandwagons in smoke-filled rooms. At present we lack the theoretical structures that would let us think clearly about this subject.

Third and finally, there will be no escaping from the need for more evidence. Until this year's primaries, nearly all primary voter samples have been national. Researchers have been forced to use samples collected for other purposes and trick them into answering their questions, as with Bartels, Brady, and Hagen, or to collect their own data, as with Stone, Abramowitz and Rapoport. With occasional exceptions like Stone and his colleagues', no large academic datasets have been collected from states during their primaries. This has been an enormous barrier to research. For example, it has made it impossible to say whether voters were uninformed when they voted or only when they were not personally faced with a choice. The new National Election Study from the Michigan group should make possible an answer to that question, and to many others as well.

In addition, theoretical notions (including my own fancies in this essay) are all too easily produced and too easily believed without the constraint of empirical testing. We will need more intensive case studies of the sort Fenno has done, more comparative historical studies such as Polsby's, along with more statistically oriented work such as that by Stone and his colleagues, Hagen, Bartels, and Brady. Each of these can help test their own interpretations and explanations; they can also tell us how well our more formalized theories are working and how much understanding remains outside our formalisms.

In short, as a profession we continue to struggle for a clear theoretical understanding and defensible democratic evaluation of the primary process. But our progress has been marked. And the work represented in the other chapters of this book not only demonstrates how far we have come, but suggests that Charles Merriam's vision of a scientific social science that would serve the cause of mass democracy might yet be realized.

Notes

1. Note that whether or not to have a plebiscite is one issue; whether to include all adults in a given plebiscite is another. In my view the latter is a much easier question. In particular, exclusion of women and minorities from participation in party affairs is indefensible.

2. Bagehot (1966, p. 81) concedes that Lincoln was "if not of eminent ability, yet of eminent justness," and that he represented a certain "success in a lottery."

3. This argument justifies neither arbitrarily heavy coverage of unfamiliar candidates, nor uniformly uncritical and laudatory coverage of early winners. The media can be criticized on both scores in 1984.

References

Arrow, Kenneth J. 1963. *Social Choice and Individual Values*. New York: Wiley. (Original work published in 1951.)

Bagehot, Walter. 1966. *The English Constitution.* Ithaca, NY: Cornell University Press. (Original work published in 1867.)

Beer, Samuel H. 1966. *British Politics in the Collectivist Age.* New York: Knopf.

Bentley, Arthur F. 1908. *The Process of Government.* Chicago: University of Chicago Press.

Brady, Henry E. 1984. Knowledge, Strategy, and Momentum in Presidential Primaries. Presented at the Weingart Conference, California Institute of Technology, Pasadena, California.

————. 1988. The Dimensions of Presidential Preferences. Unpublished manuscript.

Fenno, Richard F., Jr. 1988. Down and Out in Iowa: The 1984 Glenn Campaign. Presented at the University of Iowa Shambaugh Conference, "First in the Nation: Iowa and the Presidential Nomination Process," Iowa City, Iowa.

Harsanyi, John. 1977. *Rational Behavior and Bargaining Equilibrium in Games and Social Situations.* Cambridge: Cambridge University Press.

Lengle, James I. 1981. *Representation and Presidential Primaries: The Democratic Party in the Post-Reform Era.* Westport, CT: Greenwood Press.

Polsby, Nelson W. 1983. *Consequences of Party Reform.* New York: Oxford.

Ranney, Austin. 1954. *The Doctrine of Responsible Party Government.* Urbana, IL: University of Illinois Press.

————. 1972. Turnout and Representation in Presidential Primary Elections. *American Political Science Review,* 66:21–37.

Rousseau, Jean Jacques. 1947. *The Social Contract.* New York: Hafner. (Original work published in 1762.)

Schattschneider, E. E. 1942. *Party Government.* New York: Farrar and Rinehart.

Schelling, Thomas C. 1978. *Micromotives and Macrobehavior.* New York: W. W. Norton.

Schumpeter, Joseph A. 1942. *Capitalism, Socialism and Democracy.* New York: Harper.

Truman, David B. 1971. *The Governmental Process,* 2nd ed. New York: Knopf.

List of Contributors

Alan I. Abramowitz, *Emory University*

Christopher H. Achen, *University of Chicago*

Larry M. Bartels, *University of Rochester*

Henry E. Brady, *University of Chicago*

Michael G. Hagen, *University of California, Berkeley*

Nelson W. Polsby, *University of California, Berkeley*

Ronald B. Rapoport, *College of William and Mary*

Peverill Squire, *University of Iowa*

Walter J. Stone, *University of Colorado*

Raymond E. Wolfinger, *University of California, Berkeley*

Index